DISTINCTIVE
worship

How a new generation
connects with God

[Andy Flannagan]

with extra material on
www.youthwork.co.uk/resources/

Authentic

SPRING HARVEST
Equipping the Church for action

First published 2004 by
Spring Harvest Publishing Division and Authentic Media
9 Holdom Avenue, Bletchley, Milton Keynes, Bucks, MK1 1QR, UK
and 129 Mobilization Drive, Waynesboro, GA 30830-4575, USA
www.authenticmedia.co.uk

British Library Cataloguing in Publication Data
A catalogue record for this book is available from the British Library

ISBN 1-85078-600-3

Typeset by Spring Harvest
Cover design by Sam Redwood
Print management by Adare Carwin
Printed and bound by J.H. Haynes & Co., Sparkford

About the author

Andy Flannagan is British Youth For Christ's national songwriter/performer and worship leader. He does exactly what it says on the tin, except he also trains and resources people all over the UK to do the same. Andy has a God-given passion to communicate, and that led him to leave his job as a hospital doctor in Northern Ireland to run YFC's itinerant band TVB for three years. Since then he has been regularly performing and leading worship at events, including Spring Harvest, Summer Madness, Greenbelt and New Wine, while also leading youth worship and mentoring young leaders in his adopted home of Luton.

His songs have been used on BBC TV and radio and he even admits to a performance on Big Breakfast. Youth workers across the country have benefited from Andy's specific calling to minister in worship to 'the real heroes' through conferences, retreats and training days.

The last few years have, in Andy's words, seen 'God taking me beyond my guitar' to the forefront of developing and implementing innovative worship ideas for young people. In 2004 he released a critically acclaimed album, *SON* – 'A creative triumph from the versatile Mr Flannagan,' Tony Cummings, *Cross Rhythms Magazine*.

His attitude that we are called to 'write next year's headlines by what we do today' sums up the desire in him to see young Christians shape a culture rather than just create their own. Throw in a passion for global justice, voiced through his work with Tearfund, songs with a political edge that have bent the ears of MPs and a large dollop of playing cricket, and you have a pretty good taste of Andy's life.

Contents

Foreword

What comes into your mind when you think about God?

Our answer to this question will, as AW Tozer says, illuminate the nature of our faith.

It seems to me to be the fundamental question that all of us (whoever we are, whatever we do) must ask ourselves. Often. Because how we see God directly effects how we live.

This is certainly true in the life of dynamic Andy Flannagan.

I first met Andy in his second year of running YFC's itinerant band TVB. His pastoral heart was immediately apparent. He has a natural gift of precisely tapping into the mind-set of youth – band members and young people in the community alike.

The fruits of this book have definitely been born out of years of grassroots, hands on application. Andy's genuine dedication to everything he does has led to an abundance of innovative ideas.

The last few years have seen him at the forefront of developing and implementing ground-breaking worship ideas for young people.

It is our responsibility to seek out and explore authentic expressions of communication with this generation. To some of us this may seem an impossible task, but we've been asked, indeed commanded, to go and make disciples of all nations – and such a command wasn't exclusively directed to people over a certain age. Therefore it is our duty to explore ways in which we can truly connect. It is our duty to find the balance between being culturally relevant and compromising the true nature – the majesty and awesomeness – of God.

In the following inspiring chapters Andy Flannagan explores various forms of worship, and through practical application encourages youth workers and all those involved with young people to engage creatively.

Instead of squeezing this generation into a pattern that is alien to their life experience, Andy gives example upon example of how a young person can be liberated and therefore drawn closer to Jesus by creating a way of life that fits the people rather than making some predestined structure that imposes on them a way of relating to the Father.

Essentially it is Andy's desire to see young Christians shape a culture rather than just shape their own

This is a great handbook – one to pick up and use time and time again.

Amidst some real nuggets of brilliance, Andy never loses sight of the overriding purpose of worship – our critical relationship with the 'ultimate lover.'

Diane Louise Jordan
Speaker/TV and Radio Presenter

Preface

This is a distinctive generation of young people. A generation that thinks, acts and speaks like no other. To paraphrase Emily from Bagpuss – I love them. This may be because I cling to the belief that I am still one of them (although I guess the Bagpuss reference has given me away!). My prayer is for *Distinctive Worship* to be a useful tool that empowers youth workers to think about some of the distinctives of culture that impact on worship and some of the distinctives of worship that need to impact a culture. I hope these distinctives inform our thinking and practice as we seek to facilitate worship for this generation.

Much of what I've experienced has been through the privilege of working for British Youth For Christ, where I spent three years leading their itinerant band TVB. Since then I have been leading worship, writing songs, and resourcing and training others in these areas. I want to take this opportunity to thank all the folks from YFC and ONE[1] (my church) who have taught me so much throughout this time. Thanks also to the young people of Luton and Portadown, whose lives and honesty have inspired much of what is on these pages. This is also the place to note that much of what I have been allowed to experience pleasantly has been through the blood, sweat and tears of phenomenal local youth workers, whose passion and dedication never cease to remind me why I do what I do.

Regarding the logistics of getting the book together, I am indebted to the following folks: Marion Williams, Tim Hewitt, Christine Macfie, Tim Malcolm, Barry Mason, Dave Steell, but most of all to Jude Smith without whom this simply would not have happened.

These people in particular have shaped and encouraged my thinking in this area; Roy Crowne, Russell Rook, Tim Hewitt, Jude Smith and Phil Glover. Thanks also to Spring Harvest and the Youthwork – the partnership team for the opportunity to do this in the first place.

Andy Flannagan
August 2004

'... do not try to call them back to where they were, and do not try to call them to where you are, beautiful as that place may seem to you. You must have the courage to go with them to a place that neither you nor they have been before.'

Vincent Donovan

Introduction

Dave was a studious little man of twelve going on thirty-something. He would often sit on his own, happily reading and thinking. A classic teacher's pet, Dave had grown up with Christianity all around him and accepted it as just another set of facts to be understood and learnt like all the others he loved to digest. Singing Christian songs was a regular part of his life because that was what you did; but it had no more significance than the other things he just did, like cleaning his teeth. One summer, everything changed. Dave was at a camp, which he thought a funny thing to call it when you were sleeping in school classrooms. After a long day of activity, he would sit with everyone else as a man with gold-rimmed glasses and a guitar led them in songs. This was neither particularly novel, nor exciting. Towards the end of the week, however, Dave noticed that the words he was singing were written as if someone was listening to them. 'This might be a bit more entertaining if I actually sing these words *to* someone,' he thought. He tried it. He liked it. When you sang the words *to* someone, it felt as if they were there. Hang on, he knew *who* was there. In one explosive moment the facts long stored in his head collided at great speed with this new experience and the product was worship.

Dave was actually called Andy, and twenty years later I find myself wandering through the Arndale shopping centre in my hometown. This is my essential, regular reality check. My eyes take in all that stimulates and entices this generation, and my heart breaks as I observe young people engaged in a lifelong performance to an ever more demanding crowd. Yet my mind recalls the awesome moments of intimacy and power I have shared with young people in worship. I ask myself: 'Can these two worlds ever connect, like mine suddenly did?' I do know one thing; they desperately need to. I want to be involved with worship that *all* this generation can enter into; not just the two per cent of them who like me have grown up in church.

It feels as if those involved in preaching have effectively grasped the nettle of postmodernism and a rapidly evolving youth culture, for instance in their use of story and imagery. But have we who seek to facilitate worship sat on our comfortable laurels and instead created a world of our own? A world much easier to control, but irrelevant to a young person entering the real world. Young people operate in a culture barely recognisable as what I knew twenty years ago, so the section 'Distinctives of where we are' explores key shifts in areas such as reverence, leadership, family and imagery, and how these inform the way we facilitate and lead worship. Stumbling onto these areas has revolutionised much of my thinking with regard to working with young people. The section 'Distinctives of where we could be' examines the distinctives integral to effective work with this generation, such as experience, community and creativity. 'Mechanics of Distinctive Worship' gives practical advice in areas such as band and crowd dynamics.

Informed by the previous sections, 'Ideas for Distinctive Worship' contains 75 worship ideas that have worked really well for us in Luton and all over the country. These will be of use in small or large group settings.

I have a dream that when someone sits down to look at these issues again in twenty years time they will find a reverse process has occurred. I pray that instead of finding that our young people's worshipping lives have been ever more shaped by their culture, they will find that the vitality and reality of worship have impacted a culture to a point where it is unrecognisable.

To change a culture, however, you have to engage with it, so let's look into the fascinating spiritual, physical, emotional and mental dynamics at play when this generation worships. I hope we'll find a script for the privileged role of facilitating the first moments of a lifetime of worship.

SORRY
I love you

Sorry

Thank you

I love you

thank you
sorry

I love you

thank you
sorry

Chapter 1

Horizontal and Vertical

Doing youthwork you quickly realise there are certain phrases that teenagers (or any of us) find especially hard to say. The main three that spring to mind are:

- Sorry
- Thank You
- I Love You.

If it's a struggle for young people to get these words travelling horizontally to their peers, how much harder is it for to them address these phrases vertically to God? This is of crucial importance, because when you think about it those three phrases sum up a sizeable chunk of our worship vocabulary.

[Sorry]

In a society where young people are subliminally trained not to be vulnerable, 'sorry' really does seem to be the hardest word. Conflict resolution is mostly carried out by way of argument, and survival is definitely for the fittest. Set in this context, the repentance involved in worship needs some serious explaining; especially how you could have the nerve to do it publicly, even if in the odd moment of honesty you can achieve it in private.

My upbringing in Northern Ireland illuminates this issue. There are exceptions of course, but in general because of our history no one admits to being wrong since this would be an admission that the other side is right. Part of the reason it is so hard to say 'sorry' is that it involves an assumption that you are giving ground to an enemy. If we can instil in young people the truth – yes, there is someone who is always right but he is on our side – then an interesting shift in mindset can occur. This is aided when they find that the one who is always right, always loves. When we use the song 'Surrender' with young people I often remind them that we are not surrendering at the point of a gun to an enemy, but to our closest friend. The recipient of our apology won't gloat or remind us of our mistakes. For some young people this doesn't ring true. A person who makes the laws yet acts with love is a person they have never known in their family, at school or in the justice system.

In many of the young people I have worked with (and I often see it in myself) a switch is tripped when they are accused of something. 'Deny everything' is the automatic response. Shaggy summed up this blame-free culture with his generic get-out clause – 'It wasn't me!' God isn't content, thankfully, to leave things this way.

> *But God demonstrates his own love for us in this: While we were still sinners, Christ died for us.*
>
> Romans 5:8

In other words, while we are still in denial, protesting our innocence, the innocent one is hanging there, proclaimed guilty. The scale of this injustice is sometimes the only thing that can break through the wall of denial and bring someone to the point where they say 'sorry'.

The spectre of relativism floats into our discussion here. Many before me have proven how it has become the accepted doctrine of our culture. Amongst young people, there is little analysis of the contradictions in a relativistic way of thinking. Their lack of conflict resolution skills extends to mental conflicts. It is much handier for someone to be allowed to have their truth and for me to have mine. The lack of absolute standards makes it easier to engage in moral contortionism, so I can justify whatever feels good at this moment. You can appreciate the mental leap required to get from here to a point of saying sorry for anything. If something is not actually wrong, just one out of many interesting choices that differ only in their shades of grey, then it makes no sense to confess it as by nature sinful.

To address this, we use ideas that involve listing the fruits of the spirit while also listing sins that people may want to get rid of. These words can be written on pieces of paper and scattered over the floor, then people pick them up to keep or put in a trash can. Stimulating our consciences by listing what we may have done right and wrong helps to set the bar. People left to conjure up their own confessions often sit there thinking that 'actually, I'm all right'. See 'Help me hold on' on Page 170 in the Ideas Section.

Some people need to meet the all-perfect being face to face before they can realise that we all fall appallingly short of perfection. If we facilitate worship experiences that deny space and time for young people to commune with their maker, we are in danger of creating experiences that do little but restate theology. When the Holy Spirit is given free reign to convict people of sin, change can occur many times faster than if we solely continually restate the truth of their sin to them. The bright purity of God so outdoes anything we can make with our fancy gadgets and clever visuals. Bring it on, God.

[Thank You]

As a society, over the last twenty years we have shifted from fulfilling our responsibilities towards claiming our rights. Listen to a young person demanding some action from their mobile phone company. You will hear a highly developed awareness of their rights and a vicious attitude towards obtaining them. Compare that energy to the inertia when it is suggested they look after a younger brother or sister. I know where they learned this. From us. So no casting stones. If you believe you receive most things as a divine right, you have no reason to say 'thank you' for them.

> If the vertical arm is broken we are left with experience for the sake of it, and if the horizontal arm is broken we are no more than wannabe angels.

I love the young lads I play cricket with. I enjoy being a part-time taxi service for away games. I can count on one hand the number of times I have been thanked for doing the driving, even though the journeys are usually pretty eventful! This doesn't bother me, but it shows a mindset. The lift is just another thing this world owes them. This lack of appreciation or gratitude informs so much of young people's attitudes to their families and the planet. They are used to simply getting what they pay for. Why say thanks? That's what the shop is there for, isn't it?

When young people encounter grace, that's when things begin to change. I normally don't win competitions, but one summer I won two tickets to watch England play Pakistan at the Oval. Fantastic!

I was gutted to find out that on the day of the game I would be in Norway. So I gave the tickets to two lads from the team and didn't think much more about it. The next week at practice I was apprehended by a crowd of the lads basically saying: 'You nutter. You could have got over a hundred quid for those.' And other 'polite' words to that effect. I said I just wanted to give the tickets to them, but it didn't register. It blew me away that someone giving something away for no personal gain had messed with their heads so much. The guys really enjoyed the match, and sent me many texts in Norway saying thank you. When young people start to experience the grace of God through us and from each other, those words can appear.

[I Love You]

It often begins as a cheap phrase but ends up being very costly. The rejection a young person often feels after hearing the words 'I love you' makes the sentiment seem either fickle or painful. All of us, young people included, are experts at assembling complex barriers that prevent anyone getting close enough to hurt us again – and often this includes God. Our fear of intimacy can take a long time to overcome.

> The experience of worship is simultaneously making connections to our earthly daily experience and heavenly spiritual reality.

I long to see young people released into the fullness of intimate worship. I desperately desire for them to know the totality of relationship that Jesus offers. But the further I journey alongside young people, both in Ireland and England, the more I realise that so little of what holds them back is to do with what is happening in a room and so much is to do with what is going on inside them. The conflicts, the still-believed lies about themselves, the feelings of shame from abusive situations, and the inability to accept unconditional love are just some of the things that prevent a deep worship relationship. Issues around the words 'I love you' are just the tip of an emotional iceberg.

It has been amazing in Luton to see many young people released from the 'stuff' of the past that invades the present. The role of this book is not to go into the details of the ministry involved in seeing restoration and healing in these young people, but worship has a key role to play.

Periods of resting in God's presence combined with truth spoken in love to those old situations are often the triggers to free people. After a recent worship session we received an amazing email from a girl who had never been able to forgive a bloke who had treated her abusively.

> *Suddenly it was like a light switched on inside me. I realised that I truly didn't want to carry these things around any more and that even though what he had done to me was wrong, I didn't need to keep being angry about it, that I wanted to make my own (very small) attempt to live out the grace of Jesus by letting it go and forgiving him. That night I used the response exercise with the stones to do this and also received prayer about it for the first time. Since then I've felt so much better.*

The exercise she mentioned involves writing on stones all the reasons why we could blame folks for what they did to us. This is based on the story of the woman caught in adultery from John 8. In that story, Jesus was the only one who could have justifiably thrown a stone at her; yet he relinquished his rights and responded in grace. So instead of throwing the stones, we dropped them in a pile that formed an altar to remind us of God's grace.

We develop the freedom to love as we begin to understand we are loved unconditionally, but it is hard for young people to believe this is when the exact opposite is modelled to them by soap opera, celebrity and family relationships. It seems that love comes with many strings attached, to be snapped at any moment if the going gets tough.

A young person's belief that they are unlovable is a lie that obstructs the process. A truth that speaks powerfully into this situation is Psalm 149:3–4.

> *Let them praise his name with dancing and make music to him with tambourine and harp. For the LORD takes delight in his people; he crowns the humble with salvation.*

For many young people it is a revelation that they could be significant enough to God to bring him pleasure. He must love them.

Nothing fills me with more joy than meeting folks who have truly grasped this unconditional love and are learning to walk in it. You see, it's not just a nice idea to make worship more meaningful. It genuinely changes a person's whole outlook on life. Chronic attention-grabbing behaviour recedes when you know you have someone's attention permanently. There is a shift from the desperation of offering yourself cheaply in the hope of being loved, to knowing that you are loved.

> We possess integrity because we have crafted our worship experiences to be a continuation of the challenge of our lives, rather than an escape from it – keeping our feet on the earth, but our head in the clouds.

To persist with one-size-fits-all worship just hoping all these issues get sorted out in the fullness of time is to live in cloud cuckoo land. Worship is a powerful place where God can shine truth into the dark places of the soul, and as leaders we shouldn't be scared to confront these things head on.

[Summary]

As well as presenting an awesome challenge, I believe our situation presents a phenomenal opportunity. In today's youth culture(s) the community and intimacy that worship can foster are exactly what are needed, and needed desperately. It is perhaps the vertical articulation of words of regret, passion and thanks that will create the vulnerability and confidence needed for deeper horizontal interactions.

Time and time again we see young people transformed as interactors by their experience of God in worship. The generation summed up by the word 'what-everrr!' begins to see who and why. Defences built over years of self-protection crumble and the old person is barely recognisable. Words of encouragement and physical contact enter the vocabulary of folks you thought could never express themselves in those ways.

[Dual Resonance]

I believe this presents us with a challenge – to create worship spaces and experiences where the horizontal and vertical planes intersect. I love facilitating dual resonance, where the imagery, music, people, objects and actions people encounter in worship all have a resonance with both heaven and earth. If the vertical arm is broken we are left with experience for the sake of it, and if the horizontal arm is broken we are no more than wannabe angels.

This means that when we harp on and on about worship being a life, not an event, we speak with some integrity and reality. We possess integrity because we have crafted our worship experiences to be a continuation of the challenge of our lives, rather than an escape from it – keeping our feet on the earth, but our head in the clouds. The experience of worship is simultaneously making connections to our earthly daily experience and heavenly spiritual reality.

That's probably how the disciples felt in the midst of their intensely horizontal, yet intensely vertical, worship experiences with Jesus. There was horizontality in their sense of community and the use of 'stuff of earth' such as bread and wine. Vertically they were in no doubt that they were connecting to the divine, experiencing the supernatural, and being changed internally. You will find these two axes informing many of the ideas as we move through this book.

My boss, Jon, is always talking about the theology of sprouts. He believes we avoid awkward tasks in the same way that we push sprouts around a plate, leaving them to last in the hope that we won't have room for them. In 'Distinctives of where we are' (Chapters 3 to 9) we will look at more of the distinctives of young people and their culture, but for now let's close our eyes, grab a fork and get straight to the area of worship that seems to give youth workers most trauma.

Chapter 2

Unchurched?

Youth workers often ask something like this: 'We can get them in okay. They enjoy the activities and listen to the talks really well, but it seems as if they struggle to step up to the "next level" of actually worshipping. How can we make it happen?'

There is no easy answer. Some of the thoughts in this chapter focus on activities that connect with a young person's experience, helping to build bridges. It is harder to engage someone in meaningful worship if they don't believe in God or have no relationship with him, but in my experience worship is often a vital part of their journey towards God rather than just something that gets activated when they become a Christian.

You may already be living with the tension of making worship 'accessible' to unchurched young people in your area without losing the distinctives of what you have developed as a worshipping community. I have chatted to many frustrated youth workers who feel that their efforts to include those on the fringes, or even beyond the fringes, have left those at the centre neglected.

It is comforting to know that Jesus faced similar challenges. He certainly started with a strong core of close followers, but there was never a time when his methods of interaction were alien to those outside his inner sanctum. Jesus frequently went out of his way to commune with those on the edge, and no other passion seems to get as much story-telling airtime. Evidence for the prosecution; the parables of the lost son, sheep, and coin. I'm pretty sure that not many management gurus would advise a strategy such as that of the shepherd in the parable of the lost sheep. I suspect the hundredth sheep would be written off as natural wastage so that the ninety-nine didn't suffer from lack of attention. God doesn't see things that way. He sees a big difference between the ninety-nine and the one – the ninety-nine aren't lost.

[Differentiation]
Differentiated activities are a tool teachers use to get a class engaged in the same overall activity, but at a level appropriate to their ability. Similarly, we need to foster differentiated worship so young people are able to find their own depth whether they have never been near a church or have spent their whole life there. Creative involvement, as shown in the examples later, is crucial to making this work.

[Passions]
Youth For Christ workers and associates have much experience working with unchurched teenagers, especially through Rock Solid clubs – themed hi-energy games-based programmes for 11–14-year-olds. In helping these young people towards faith, we have discovered that allowing their passions to lead our thinking regarding worship is essential.

For example: making space for young people to bring in their favourite music and asking them to say why they like it. This gives you a feel for where they are at emotionally, spiritually and musi-cally, and draws them into a pattern of participation. As discussion develops, you can introduce music for worship that connects with their sensibilities.

[Creativity]
Wherever they are on their journey toward God, a young person is human and has the image of God imprinted in them. I marvel at the colossal creativity of artists, musicians and film-makers who would not claim any connection with God. Like it or not, we all have something of his creative nature in us. I believe releasing the God-given creativity of unchurched young people is a fantastic step towards them connecting with God. Whether they know it or not, as their creativity is awakened they are connecting with something of God in themselves. This often kick-starts a process through which they come to realise that they are born to be with God.

Here are some thoughts on ways to release this creativity.

[Rap]
Some young people will write raps when they would never dream of writing anything else. At Youth For Christ we have seen the fruit of this in our work in Young Offender Institutions (YOI). I will never forget my first morning at Castington YOI. About fifteen

lads paraded in with the classic 'hard' exterior, warning me I was on their turf and we would be playing by their rules! Their carefully placed verbal darts flew for a few minutes, only to be displaced by looks of utter disbelief as they realised the strange Irish guy was actually suggesting they could create something worthwhile and that someone would listen to it! At first it was about as hard as not just getting blood out of a stone but also miraculously transfusing it into bodies close to death. Given a blank page, people will often struggle, but supply direction and themes and eventually brains get moving. You can spot pretty quickly who will be most creative if left to get on with it, and who needs the stimulus of a group of two or three others to encourage the process. Persistence and patience are key here.

> People need to know that it is OK to worship God from where they are right now rather than feeling they must wait until they feel or look sorted.

The right starting point is also crucial. Geoff, the YFC prison worker, had told us that the young people were really into hip-hop and hard house so we decided to engage them in writing raps and programming tracks. We were speaking a language they could understand.

We gave them the theme of 'hope' and started by discussing as a group what that word meant to them. Then we brainstormed words they associated with hope. The word 'hope' triggers some interesting thoughts when someone is locked away, and it was a real privilege to see the guys start to open up. By the second session, some of the lads were volunteering their dreams for a new life 'outside'. This level of vulnerability was impossible a day earlier, when any such statement would have been immediately shot down as fantasy or pathetic sentimentality (but probably not in those words).

Some of the guys actually made the connection between what they were talking about and eternal hope, i.e. that being locked in Castington with the hope of getting out was not unlike being stuck on this planet with the hope of heaven. But many clung to a presumption that things were never going to get better – that they were trapped on a street that was headed only one way. Words eventually flowed; words of real frustration, words that I wouldn't repeat, words that painted a dark but honest picture of the inside of their cells and, more importantly, the inside of their heads and hearts.

We were using simple computer programs to create backing tracks for the raps they had written, and words that had just been scribbles on a page sprang into life. The shift in energy and focus was palpable. Even the completely disinterested members of the group were contributing now. The steps that these guys were taking were small, but significant; connecting with each other, connecting with their own feelings and articulating them rather than (as normal) letting them bubble up inside with disastrous consequences. I share this story as an example of how folks who might seem far off actually begin to connect when given the tools in a format and language they understand.

With your young people, the lyrics won't start out looking like Psalm 23 (I wonder what David's first efforts were like), but with your influence and the influence of others around them you may well be surprised. If you want the finished product to be a communal experience, you'll need to encourage folks to provide an easy spoken or sung hook where everyone can join in. Something simple and repetitive is usually best. Link these folks up with those who are into DJ-ing. They may have hip-hop or ambient tracks that provide plenty of space for some MC-ing action.

[Rhythm]

> *Our world is full of rhythm. Its whole motion is rhythmic, and wherever you find life you find rhythm. The first introduction to God in scripture is in Genesis 1:2 '... the Spirit of God was hovering over the waters.' He set the world in motion, and as he breathed life into man, he set us in motion within it. God has used rhythm as a core ingredient in all things.*
>
> *from www.psalmdrummers.org*

Rhythm, everyone can enjoy being part of it. As with creativity, rhythm is core to the human experience; our hearts beating, our eyes blinking, our steps carrying us down a street. We cannot avoid connecting with what we know is innately part of us, whether we acknowledge that it is from God or not. We continually experience rhythmic events from outside ourselves; waves crashing on a shore, washing machines vibrating, pneumatic drills, birdsong, ringtones, car alarms – the list is endless. This is why rhythm is one of the most natural mediums in which to express yourself, and why some people find it a more natural communal medium than singing.

At Christmas in Luton thousands of busy shoppers tramp wearily around the pedestrian precinct. The pavement is a partner in a non-stop rhythm of consumerism. Every store threatens injury from repetitive strains of Christmas musak, which like the rhythm of the Irish Sea is more than slightly nauseating. Today the Psalm Drummers are in town as part of an all-day carol service. People who wandered by during many of the other sessions are drawn to the rhythm. A large crowd gathers, intrigued and entertained. Watching from a distance, I sense rather than see something unusual happening. Almost imperceptibly at first, the static crowd is beginning to move. First a finger, then a foot, then an outrageous shoulder. Just for a moment, shopping bags are dropped. There is something infectious about the rhythm; something that is connecting people to the groove and its creators. Could it be that the creator of rhythm is drawing people to himself?

After some minutes a range of percussion instruments are passed around the crowd. Folks fight to get them, like shoppers racing for the bargains in a Boxing Day sale. At first everyone continues to bang out the standard rhythm that has developed, but people gradually begin to experiment with different rhythms and fills, revelling in their individual creativity. The whole thing becomes a joyous noise, and you can see and sense that people know there is more happening than the random hitting of things. You can see it in the faces of the drummers (some of who have left the stage and moved into the crowd) and feel it in the passion of the drumming.

Chip, who is leading the drummers, hops back on stage and gets folks responding to his rhythm. He beats, they beat back. Then he starts shouting words to the rhythm. Words that everyone recognises. 'Our Fa-ther who art in heaven, Hallowed be thy name!' Everyone responds in kind. We work our way through the prayer, with the crowd continuing to shout back the prayer with real intent. By the halfway stage people are feeling the freedom to dance to the groove on the fringes of the crowd.

I'm sure people prayed the Lord's Prayer that day who had never even thought of praying it before, and some found words long dormant had been powerfully reactivated. I saw in the crowd the

myriad ethnicities that make Luton the wonderful melting pot that
it is. People had been drawn in because the medium was common
to them, interactive, fun and communal. There are more ideas for
involving people with rhythmic worship on the Psalm Drummers'
website.

Rhythm-based worship is often empowering for young drummers, who can feel they don't get a chance to lead or that their desire
to beat things to death is misunderstood. Empower these folks
to develop some rhythmic worship. It is unbelievable how much
percussion gear you can accumulate by grabbing random pieces of
junk. I have seen road signs, radiators, water coolers, dustbins and
music stands used with excellent percussive purpose.

With a youth group, it is sometimes best to introduce the use
of rhythms as worship in a sung worship time. It is helpful to split
a group into three sections, each following someone who can
strongly bang or clap out a rhythm. Choose three rhythms that
will work during a song, and teach these to the three leaders. Then
in 'breakdown' sections of songs, the leaders have the freedom to
kick off their rhythm with their group following. There is a real joy
as the rhythms play off each other, and combine to create a more
complex rhythm. After some time, you can begin singing again on
top of the rhythm. Quite a sight and quite a sound. Joyful noise can
also be skilful noise.

[Physical Movement]
When working with the 11–14 age group, much of the connection we have achieved has been via modern physical movement
in songs. If you can keep the movements non-cheesy they are a
fantastic way of engaging this age group. Sadly we are often scared
away from using actions in songs because of the lingering negative
associations of children's songs. Here are two examples. In a song
called 'Around', as the young people sing 'round, and around, and
around again' they bounce and spin, first one way then the other.
During other sections they hand-jive and make statues. The frenzy
of the chorus is exhilarating, and even the most uninterested lads
at the back end up joining in. This has often been a key moment
when they start to engage in worship. Another song, called 'The
Reason', has folks getting down on the floor in preparation for a
Mexican wave (or two) as the chorus approaches. If you can attach

the movement to the theme, these are the songs that young people remember years later.

[Rage Against the Machine]

There is an opportunity in the midst of the potentially worrying explosion of parental advisory material in music in the last few years. The uncompromising but honest lyrics being articulated by nu-metal bands and controversial rap artists can be used constructively when encouraging lyric writing. So many of the lyrics are shouting rage at some 'system' or 'structure', but when you ask what that entity is it's hard to get definite answers. There seems to be some nebulous fog out there that everyone is mad at. What if the counter-cultural desires of those who listen to these artists could be channelled positively? Why not encourage these guys to direct their anger at someone who's really there. We've had 14-year-olds do this, and be surprised when we've told them that they have just written their first psalm. For some it is the first step towards faith. Giving some context to this honesty and anger opens up a line of communication that is often reactivated at a later date. There is good biblical precedent for directing your anger, apathy or frustration at God. Look at Psalm 22:1.

> *My God, my God, why have you forsaken me?*
> *Why are you so far from saving me,*
> *so far from the words of my groaning?*

Somehow we have sanitised these words, removing their gut-wrenching reality. My suspicion is that if we heard a metal band growling or wailing the above lyrics, we would probably be questioning their suitability for our young people's ears. We would possibly also be offended that someone in a position of influence was publicly questioning God's credentials. Yet the amazing upside-down truth is that these words were not too abrasive for Jesus to quote on the cross.

And there's more…

> *Why, O Lord, do you stand far off?*
> *Why do you hide yourself in times of trouble?*
>
> *Psalm 10:1*

Awake, O Lord! Why do you sleep?
Rouse yourself! Do not reject us for ever.
Why do you hide your face
and forget our misery and oppression?

Psalm 44:23–24

These words aren't just plaintive pleading, they are downright accusation. There is an implication that God intentionally makes himself scarce when his people most need him, or that he is the one who is responsible for all the heartache.

> David used everyday events and language to communicate his feelings to God.

The bottom line is that David and Israel didn't make it through because they watched their language, but because they stayed in communication with God even when it meant hurling some serious abuse. From my reading of the book of Psalms, it seems that these guys would have struggled with our modern notion that negative life circumstances can be a reason for not interacting with God. I think they realised that it was all part of the deal. It may help to articulate some modern day phrases akin to those in the Psalms. Written today young people would be more likely to say.

God, what are you playing at?
Have you not noticed what is going on down here?
Are you too busy playing Big Brother to help me out?
Do you not see what they do to me?
I bet you don't even know my name anymore, do you?
Get off your backside and do something.

You may struggle reading some of that, but those phrases are in the vicinity of what David was writing. So let's broaden our minds, and encourage young people to express themselves in his direction. God is big enough to take it.

[Pop Fog]
You can apply the same thinking with that other massive section of 11–14-year-olds – pop fans. Here you have millions of young people singing along to songs in their bedrooms that are aimed at

a fantasy girl or guy, who probably doesn't even exist in the mind of the songwriter. In songwriting workshops, when young people write lyrics there seems to be a desire to connect to someone that they cannot quite describe, cannot quite touch and more than usually cannot quite have. People seem to find comfort in being able to direct their thoughts towards someone, even if that someone is unobtainable. What about suggesting that they write words that express something towards someone who does exist, who knows that they exist, and who will actually answer them? Time and time again this has been a way in for God to prove that he is a much more reliable lover than any of the fantasy projections of pop lyrics.

[Psalm Writing]

For those who have travelled a bit further, we have found the down-to-earth language of the Psalms in Eugene Peterson's *The Message* really useful in giving young people the confidence and freedom to articulate what they are feeling without having to come up with spiritual sounding words. They release young people into honesty as they realise that they are not the first to struggle with these issues and it doesn't disqualify them from worshipping. Read a psalm aloud (perhaps with some rhythm) and then encourage people to write one themselves – one blank sheet of A4 seems to work well. Ask them to tell God exactly what they are thinking; whether they happen to be hurt, frustrated, doubting or on top of the world. This is often the easier part, with the more difficult part being encouraging them to tell God what they are thinking or feeling about him.

You may have to underline the large extent to which David used everyday events and language to communicate his feelings to God. Some may want to keep their psalm private between themselves and God, but some may want to share what they have written. These could be woven into a communal time of sung worship. However don't mention this before they begin writing as it tends to influence the extroverts to write things that people will want to hear as opposed to what they honestly want to express to God. Ensure that the first few psalms read to the group leave room for folks to read negative psalms without feeling they are disappointing anyone with their 'lack of faith'.

In an attempt to get your own creative juices flowing, here is a psalm that I wrote last year. For once my pen got to the paper before

my brain could protest with its usual platitudes and spin doctoring.
This came straight from the horse's mouth and heart.

Psalm

This is great Lord
This life just gets better and better.
Not easier, but better and better.
But I want to get better and better too.

I think I see two modes to my life, Lord;
Seeking and stumbling.
And I know that I learn from the falling, but would you
help me spot the tripwires?
Give me your infrared vision to spot those red lasers of
temptation.

I'll be more honest with you and my mates – more current
with you – more Five Live and less Daily Telegraph.

I want lots of short Internet accounts with you, not one big
TESSA that I never touch.

You do know best, and I love the fact that as well as crying
when I stumble, there is a part of you that laughs. Thank
you that you don't take me as seriously as I do.

Please explode into my consciousness with such volume,
or with such silence that I can't ignore you. Sorry that you
often have to strain your voice over the background noise,
and even then you still take "no" for an answer.

I may run away, but still the dynamic duo of Goodness
and Mercy will chase after me like Starsky and Hutch...

... all the days of my life.

Help me hear the sirens.

Son

If anyone struggles with staring at a blank page, you can helpfully use the pattern of a biblical psalm to provide a framework for them. It is easiest to see it in terms of questions. Work out what questions the psalm writer is answering in each verse, then make a list of them and let folks answer those questions for their own situation.

E.g.

How do you feel?

What is the problem?

How long has it been going on?

Who are you calling to for help?

Why does it feel as if no one cares?

Who is your helper?

What is he like?

[Home or Away?]

As most people are aware, there is something special in the dynamic of young people removed from their normal context. With the intimacy an 'away' experience brings there is a great opportunity for unchurched young people to see Christian community in action, and often the most natural expression of what is being shared together is worship. You can capitalise on the desire that suddenly springs up in even the most socially challenged of the group to want to be doing things together.

Another positive is the inherent freedom of geographical separation from issues at home or school.

[Taking Your Time]

When leading unchurched young people in sung worship we have found the best policy is, 'Don't assume too much, but don't be condescending.' Repeating some things for those in the know does no harm at all, as constant reminders eventually become good habit. Feel free to stop or stall songs if something needs explaining, or you want to encourage folks to get stuck in. Take time to repeat lines, or whole verses. Try 'hovering' (playing a repeating chord sequence) to leave space for the meaning to sink in, to explain the line, or to pray a prayer that reinforces the sense of the line.

This is a good example of the need for leadership when working with unchurched teenagers, especially in the 11–14 age group. By this I don't mean a kind of control to stunt them, but genuine leadership. Sometimes I fear that we hide behind the 'less of me, more of him' banner when this group are often just crying out to be led. Don't be afraid to think strategically about grabbing attention and engaging people. Communicate well, with an awareness of what will connect for this age group. This needs more preparation and thought than for later teens or adults. It's amazing how many of the positive emails I get about worship are not only about songs, but also the importance of the 'thought' or 'angle' dropped in before or during the worship. Supplying a conceptual hook to hang thoughts on brings focus and remembrance, and acts as a teaching tool for those just learning the ropes.

This means building up a mental library of modern pictures that help describe who God is or what worship is. I challenge you to be on the lookout for things that can describe to an unchurched young person who God is and what worship is, whether it involves mobiles, fanmail or motorways.

[All on a Plate?]

The manner of a young person's first encounter with God is significant. Our experience shows that sometimes those who have had to work a little bit harder to find what they're looking for are the ones still with God years later. This is far from a general truth, but I feel it should have some influence on our approach to leading sessions of worship for unchurched young people. This is why we should put such a premium on involvement and interaction, rather than simply polishing our product to such an extent they cannot say no. If we present every word on a plate, how can a young person develop their own vocabulary of worship? Surely the challenge is to develop this vocabulary through encouraging creativity in writing, singing, drawing, dancing and speaking. In the short-term this may lead to less of a warm fuzzy feeling, but in the long-term provide a stable framework for an individual's life of worship.

[Where are People at?]

Worship vocabulary

Most of us who grew up Christian have singing as our default form of worship expression, unaware that we actually learned that form of expression and vocabulary. We picked it up from our parents, churches and Sunday schools to the point where it feels normal to the exclusion of any other form of expression.

As with a foreign language, it takes quite some time to build up a big enough vocabulary to not feel self-conscious when using it. In a dance worship context this means moves, chants, shouts, MC-ing, and allowing shared moments to be part of a communal form of celebration. None of these may start easily or naturally, but once allowed do flow. My point is; just because something doesn't work the first time, don't give up on it. Similarly in the context of art-based work, vocabularies are built up around colours and textures, fonts and images. What you see in general is that folks who have grown up free from standard Christian programming find fewer problems in expressing themselves in these other media, and conversely find non-spontaneous group singing rather strange. We have to craft worship experiences for those whose verbal and physical vocabulary has been learnt from MTV and not Songs of Praise.

> We may discover that some of our sacred cows are just comfortable cows. In order to move towards the place your young people inhabit, you may have to leave that comfort zone just as David did.

We also need to think about where people are at spiritually. Many young people feel pretty hollow, and beneath the layers of attitude some are desperate and despairing. Jesus met many people like this and gave them the opportunity to have a real spiritual encounter. He didn't demand noise and bouncing and energy. As Sally Morgenthaler mentions in a letter on Sacramentis.com, the Samaritan woman at the well (John 4) wouldn't fit comfortably into most modern praise and worship sessions. 'He didn't ask her to be happy, to adopt religious behaviours for the sake of image, or to look in any way "together" when she clearly was not.'

Fostering openness, honesty and safe spaces where people feel able to express what they are feeling before it's sorted is vital if we are to see young people from outside the church take that road back home. It's here we need to look at our values and check if, for example, it's always the 'success' or 'high-achiever' testimonies that get included in our gatherings. People need to know that it is OK to worship God from where they are right now rather than feeling they must wait until they feel or look sorted.

It's frustrating that we seem to spend a lot of time in debates and seminars discussing 'where young people are at', but we seldom bother to ask the young people. The way they answer that question is just as informative as what they actually say. I have heard stories from youth workers who had assumed the worst about their crew, but in the end it was their young people who were coming to them to say, 'Could we take this a bit deeper?' In a group context, young people will often be scared to push out for fear of being seen as teacher's pet. But if you take the time to ask them individually, sometimes you will be blown away by the depth of what is actually ticking away in there. Young people come from so many different places, there is real profit in asking simple questions such as: 'So, what do you think worship is?' and 'What worship experiences have you been part of at school, at a church, at a youth group, or in your home?'

[Where are You at?]

With all this discussion of where young people are at, it is probably worth stopping to think about where you are at and why. In light of our 'learned vocabulary' discussion, take a moment to make an honest assessment of what your default worship mode is. We each relate to God in a way that no one else does, in a way that is innately us. We need to see which of our preferences are purely learned and habitual, and which should be non-negotiable because they are central to who we are. We may discover that some of our sacred cows are just comfortable cows. In order to move towards the place your young people inhabit, you may have to leave that comfort zone just as David did in 2 Samuel 24 (see Page 182). If you are a couple of generations beyond your young people (a generation is only five years these days) and are genuinely struggling to engage with aspects of youth culture without completely losing your personal integrity and looking relatively silly, then this is good impetus for empowering younger leaders. They will not have to think hard to start where others are at, because they are already there.

[Qs]

◉ What aspects of your present worship experiences may need 'translation' for an unchurched young person?

The next chapters focus in on some distinctives of the culture and context in which young people worship to help us further understand where they are coming from, and in the light of these things best facilitate worship for them.

Dirtbag

Setting: Youth camp – mostly unchurched young people.

Context: A complete stranger is leading worship.

The looks on the faces said it all – 'Go on, impress us'. They were mixed, half 'we don't really want to be here' and half 'this should be fun to watch'.

We had met as a band for the first time that afternoon, and I had picked up some thoughts as to where the young people were at. With this in mind, I noticed during the practice that the riff for 'Teenage Dirtbag' by Wheatus (one of the biggest chart songs at the time) bore a remarkable resemblance to something that could be used for 'Lord, I lift your Name on High' (already in *Guinness World Records* for largest number of musical stylings).

I'll never forget the looks of astonishment, and then the complete transformation from uninterested observers to full-on participants, caused by a few scratchy chords from a distinctly un-worshipful song. People were pogo-ing and smiling, but most importantly connecting. Something in them understood that I knew who they were and where they were coming from, and that maybe I could be trusted to take them on a journey to somewhere else.

The next days were littered with references to football games, nightclubs and other contexts where people celebrate, as an attempt to free people up to give all of their bodies in worship to God and build a sense of community.

Many of the young people became Christians and met with God in ways that they would never have expected. Looking back it was probably one of the most rewarding weeks of my life, when a lot of ideas suddenly intersected in the context of worship. It had become a much broader and more relevant thing.

WHERE
we are

Distinctives of

where

are

we are

where we
are

Distinctives of
where

Chapter 3

Generation Acceleration!

The reality of generational shift landed for me about five years ago. I was teaching a class on 'Jesus: Fact or Fiction?' with a YFC team. A team member suggested it was very impressive that we still talked about Jesus, even though it was over 2000 years since his birth. He was asking questions like 'Do you think we'll still be talking about the Spice Girls in even five years time?' 'No,' came the chanted replies. He pointed out that really special people may be remembered a bit longer, for example The Beatles. Everyone nodded in agreement. Then he asked, 'Or has anyone heard of Buddy Holly?' Now I'm not quite sure why he asked that question, but I don't care because I thought the answer was truly remarkable. One little lad stretched for the ceiling and said: 'Sir, sir. (pause) My dad has some of his songs on one of those big black CDs.'

> [In the midst of everything we try to do to make worship accessible to various groups of people, we could lose the thread of who it's actually designed for. Worship is for God.]

The point is, change in culture and musical styles is gathering pace exponentially. What obsesses the teenage world in May can easily be the laughing stock of September. This is especially the case with dance music, usually a good indicator of some of the edges of youth culture. The speed with which completely new marketable genres arise from subtle changes in rhythm has music marketing executives rubbing their hands with glee, and parents struggling to subsidise a passion for 'what's new'. In effect many, many temporary little subcultures are being created, in contrast to the one brand that will hold people's attention and loyalty for a long time as with Mods and Rockers.

For worship, I am passionate about using music that connects with the soul of those listening and singing. If you fail in this you lose the inherent power that God has given us in music. Some hints for doing this are in Loops (Chapter 21) on Page 155. However, I believe we can easily be led down a blind alley or two. Let me try to explain. There is now such a large spread of genres that young people 'graduate' through in their teens. For example, 20 years ago you could have picked one musical genre that would have kept most of a group of 11–16-year-olds happy. Nowadays you might hit the mark for a few, but you'd miss wildly for others.

Suppose you desire to be specifically and accurately relevant for each age group. To reproduce the different musical stylings required you would need very different environments and different musicians. With the speed of style changes, and the argument taken to its logical conclusion, we would need one congregation for 17–19-year-olds, another one for 15–16-year-olds, a separate one for 14-year-olds, one for the older 13-year-olds and one for the younger 13-year-olds! Add to that the fact you'll need to separate the 15-year-olds into the hip-hop kids, the pop kids and the nu-metal kids and you face quite a juggling act.

> [When we believe the object of the exercise is to suit us, rather than also stretch us, I believe we have lost something of what church and worship are truly meant to be.]

Where that takes us, I think you'd agree, is quite scary. Do we really believe this is what church is supposed to look like? Welcome to the dilemma of most local church worship planners. This is where we get into the political problems of keeping everyone happy, where sometimes everything becomes such a patchwork it equals nothing. If we are limited to prescriptive musical idioms, then this compromise is bound to happen. So what do we do?

Part of the problem is attitudinal. Chris Russell tells a great story about two men leaving church one Sunday morning. As they meander down the aisle, they maintain a dignified silence. However one of them uses the freedom of the open air to share his views as they trot down the steps outside. He turns to the other and says, 'You know, I didn't get much out of the worship this morning.' His friend looks blankly back at him, so he repeats himself, 'I just didn't get much out of the worship this morning.' After a moment of thought, his friend replies, 'You know, I wasn't aware it was for you.'

That story always makes me gulp hard. If you were an outsider listening to all the discussions about style, content and keeping everyone happy that grip many of our churches, you could be forgiven for thinking that worship is primarily for us. In the midst of everything we try to do to make worship accessible to various groups of people, we could lose the thread of who it's actually designed for. Worship is for God. It is giving him what he is worth, so you could almost call it a blessèd side-effect that God, in his desire for relationship, allows us so close that we cannot but be affected. 'Here is a song for the young people.' Well, no, actually it's for God. When we believe the object of the exercise is to suit us, rather than also stretch us, I believe we have lost something of what church and worship are truly meant to be. These days we assume the right to select exactly the hair colour we want, exactly the T-shirt we want, exactly the burger we want. 'Have it your way!' seems to be the slogan not just for a fast food chain, but for a generation.

[Answers?]

Allowing people to express their God-given creativity is a fantastic method of addressing some of these issues. It is a great way of doing things together in a way that everyone connects with. For example, give everyone 10 minutes to write a psalm to God on a theme that is foremost on the church's agenda such as Jesus the healer. Pardon the generalisations, but the middle-aged folks will produce a thoughtful A4 side of delicate prose, the teenagers a scratchy half-page of gut feelings or txt msg grammar on a postcard, and the eight-year-olds a scrawled sentence with a picture. You get my drift. Everyone finds their own level in an exercise that suits them perfectly, but there is still a coherency and oneness of purpose to what the congregation is doing together. You can apply the same thinking to many creative formats such as role-playing or drawing. It also asks important questions of what a church meeting looks like in logistical terms, and why it can't be something different. Do we need new buildings (not designed for control and spectating) or new ways of using our current spaces that facilitate freedom and creativity?

The crucial difference is between participating in an event and watching a highly orchestrated performance. People may join in at appropriate moments, but do they ever feel a real sense of ownership or responsibility for the direction it takes? A passion of mine is trying to redress the balance of young people's expectations regarding worship. We have unintentionally trained them to believe they have no contribution to make. A good way to break this habit is by delegating the worship section in cell groups so folks gain experience in making suggestions and preparing things for others. Young people often feel more comfortable contributing in the setting of a cell before they bring it to a larger gathering.

[Appropriate Interruption!]

While writing this section, I received a phone call from a youth worker in London. He had been commissioned to sort out something new for the 'youth service' to turn around the dire situation of having only 15 or 20 young people at a very large church. He was asking me about the possibilities of trying some dance worship. On the end of the line I had a perfect example of the dilemma that many people face. In the context of their evening service would it work to have a DJ and MC leading worship for a crowd of perhaps 700, of whom only 15 or 20 would be under 18? Could it be counter-productive, with the rest of the church feeling alienated? If it didn't work, would it put a brake on all such future efforts? Would it really work doing dance worship in a service?

> Most youth workers eventually conclude that it's easier to disciple young people through to some level of maturity in a context they can connect with, and gradually introduce them to the main congregation when they understand more of the give and take required.

The dance worship experience is at its best when you get the environment right. That means having the right lighting, the right size of room and the right physical arrangement. If used as part of an evening service, will everyone sit in rows facing the front, which is a particularly non-dance culture pattern. And even worse, will they be inhibited by chairs? Will folks be staring at the front for leadership rather than moving in their own space? Will the young people feel they are performing to entertain the crowd?

Getting back to the point of the exercise, will the setting be attractive for young people from outside the church? Will they feel a sense of belonging or ownership as a small percentage of young people in a large crowd of thirty-somethings? Will they understand this hybrid form of gathering?

Talking through these issues on the phone brought us to the point of considering whether it was worth having a separate worship event for the young people – they would know it was theirs and have the confidence to invite friends. Then it would be practical to deal with all the aforementioned issues; space, lighting, seating, etc. But this creates the problem of integrating the young people who have experienced church in this way into the 'main' congregation.

I have found that in most of these situations a pragmatic approach is best, though at times it screams against your instinct to keep the whole of the church family together. Most youth workers eventually conclude that it's easier to disciple young people through to some level of maturity in a context they can connect with, and gradually introduce them to the main congregation when they understand more of the give and take required. Of course, the young person may well attend both gatherings in any given week. This seems to help prevent the fast-burn phenomenon where young people experience something of God at a youth event and then feel moderately cheated by the experience they are presented with at 'church'.

Situations like this underline the importance of my point that interaction and creativity are key for cross-generational worship. As long as prescriptive music (or prescriptive anything) is the primary deciding factor in any worship experience, there is the potential for division.

[Middle-aged Folk for a New Generation]

Once in a while it is good to be reminded that God is much bigger than any obstacles of 'relevance' we might presume are blocking his way. We were doing a concert where a sizeable chunk of the punters were 30-somethings and older. There was an intentionally mellow, late-night acoustic vibe with cello, violin and acoustic guitar. Not really a high-energy, multi-media, fast-moving thrill ride to stimulate the younger generation.

I noticed at the start that there were quite a few young teenagers there, bustling around and generally being their lovable selves, and there was a bunch of 'geezers' right in the front row. We got to the point in the set where we sing a song called 'Open Arms' about the Prodigal Son. God had been doing powerful things through the song, so I was more than gutted when five lads just got up and walked out in the middle of it. My mind quickly went into a vicious cycle of decline; my songs aren't relevant to young people any more, my music isn't relevant to young people any more, my performance isn't relevant to young people any more, etc.

At the half-time interval I met the lady who had organised the gig and was expressing my disappointment at the walkout. She said: 'Oh, didn't you know? Those guys went out to become Christians.' Amazingly, they had decided there was no time to waste and that right there and then was the right time to 'come home'. Brilliant! It was a stirring reminder that even if I become irrelevant, God never will.

Chapter 4

Leadership

Twenty-five years ago you could have stood in front of a group of young people confident that purely because you were standing there they would follow you. Authority was assumed. No longer is this the case.

'Why should I do what she tells me?'

'In fact, why should I do what anybody tells me?'

Whether you are a traffic warden, a teacher or a prime minister, you have to work harder to convince people to do what you ask. Age, maturity and delegated responsibility no longer automatically confer respect. I'm not saying that this is all bad, but it is different. The climate in which we lead young people, or in which they lead each other, has changed.

Trust is the key. In the long term, building a relationship establishes trust and means young people are more likely to go where you lead. There is no room any more for someone whose only meaningful contact with a group is to stand in front of them. If someone encourages us to leave our worries at the cross, our response is to a large extent based on whether this is something we see them doing or it's a suggestion just for 'lesser mortals' because of our 'lack of holiness'. In a local setting, trust is developed not only by contact but also by integrity as inevitably you cannot be best friends with everyone in a group.

In his article 'Dorothy on Leadership' (originally published in *Rev Magazine*, Nov/Dec 2000) Brian McLaren likens the difference between modern and postmodern leadership to the difference between the Wizard of Oz and Dorothy. Modern leadership is all about projecting the masculine confidence of a hero who is a great problem-solver and salesman, but the wizard is a small man hidden behind a grand façade. Followers who cannot measure up to that dynamism struggle to follow. Dorothy is on a journey with fellow travellers, and is integral in the sorting out of their problems even though she doesn't claim to have all the answers. McLaren says her leadership is 'empowering, ennobling, not patronizing, paternalistic, creating dependency.' This obviously speaks into the quality needed for a relationship to have a lasting impact with young people, but also speaks to issues as diverse as room arrangements and musical style. (These are covered in other sections.) Are we speaking at people, or worshipping with them?

I think it is fair to say that though many young people do now have a vastly different attitude to authority, deep down they still desire leadership.

[Young Leaders]

The best leaders of this generation are in this generation. A good way to counteract a bad attitude to authority is to let folks be led by their peers. To make this work, however, you'll need to create a 'learning environment' where it is all right to make mistakes and encouragement is effusive. Some of us in leadership waste huge gifts of critique and analysis because we fail to combine our skills with encouragement.

All the encouraging words I received as a teenager crystallised the importance of worship, and reinforced a calling. Though I probably did not deserve them, it was mind-blowing to hear my leader tell me his talk would not have been as powerful if the worship had not prepared everyone. An oversimplification perhaps, but it was foundational in building my sense of the significance of what I was involved with. Even now, I can hear myself going 'Yeh, cool' in a blasé response, but thankfully that hasn't prevented God's words eventually sneaking through.

Let's get alongside young leaders and worship with them (even if it's just one on one) to give them the confidence and freedom to lead worship, and allow mentoring to happen naturally. I am amazed how many thoughts, scriptures and ideas used in larger group settings emerge from times of prayer and worship where perhaps just two or three people are involved. This helps build confidence into young leaders, as they will be leading folks somewhere they have already been themselves. This creates an organic desire to share, because of the impact on their own lives. The young people that are following can often sense these changes.

When I talk of 'worship leaders' I don't mean only musical worship leaders. I include all those with a specific gifting in the production of Flash and PowerPoint presentations for worship, those who enjoy administrating worship sessions through organisation and indexing, those who produce works of painted art, those who write prose and poetry, and many more. These people need mentoring and encouragement as much as musicians.

Because of what they have been conditioned to regard as worship leading, these folks falsely believe the gifts God has given them will only ever be of use in personal worship. I enjoy seeing the brightening of eye that occurs the first time others follow where their heart has led, whether by drawing with a pencil or moving their body in worship. Restricting leadership roles to the musical sphere can stifle growth and cause you to miss potential leaders, who will eventually lead in areas beyond their 'specialised subject' as they grow in confidence and maturity.

Back in the land of Oz, we should note that the postmodern leader (Dorothy) is female. Britain is increasingly a matriarchal society where youngsters are more likely to turn to a mother figure for support than a father figure. One of my biggest frustrations in working with young people involved in worship is that the latent gifting of young women currently does not have expression. I see young women stepping back because they have only seen male leadership modelled, and often they don't want to be part of something that feels alien to who they are.

We need to release them into knowing they can lead as who they are, rather than having to step into whatever mental image of leadership they have acquired. From a practical point of view there are many advantages to having girls lead worship, including simple things such as key selection. There is also the healthy connection a girl leader will make with the girls in the group. This is simply impossible when the leader is a boy.

The 'journeying with' style of leadership that Dorothy personifies is at the moment carried out better by women. I must stress, this is not a theological truth but an observation of where we are. Also, in situations where girls do not feel as musically confident as the boys we have seen useful models emerge when a girl with leadership ability is put in charge of facilitating the worship at large, coordinating the different strands of band, artistic folks, audio-visual team, etc. They set the tone for an evening, empowering others and making decisions on programme.

[Habits]

Habits tend to be caught, not taught. Whether it is your dad's smoking, your mum's ironing, or your big brother's swearing, the influence of their habits on your habits is undeniable. I have discovered that even if I give them the best seminar in the world on leading or facilitating worship, the young people we work with are far more influenced by how they see me doing it week by week. By 'doing it' I don't mean just the mechanics of leading worship, although those are inevitably picked up too. What I'm talking about are the crucial things:

- How much time you spend praying as a team. Is it 'because we should' or a priority that never gets missed?
- The level of input the team are allowed to have. Is it a dictatorship?
- The amount of encouragement team members receive.
- The methods used to solve a problem or correct a mistake.
- The amount of time given to preparation.
- Instilling a sense of worship as you practise.
- How you encourage someone to try something different.
- The attitude and respect shown the rest of the sections of an event.
- The level of cooperation and submission to overall leadership.

I must admit, I embarrass myself when I consider what habits I may be passing on.

[Integrity]

Emphasising the link between leadership and integrity is vital, especially for young males. I am constantly surprised that people do not see the link until it is pointed out to them, usually after the damage has been done. There is an inherent magnetism and charisma about many people who are thrown into this role, and rather than ignore that fact it is best to be honest and up-front about the other dynamics that are therefore at play. I have seen groups dissipate in disillusionment because it was clear to all that the 'bright young thing' in the leader's role had deficiencies in integrity, often not unrelated to his magnetic charm. This is not to say that a charismatic personality should not be in a position of leadership, but we need to be open and honest about the challenges and responsibilities of the role. The female heart and mind can find the chemical mixture of a strong leader who is also musical, who also has his worshipful sensitive side, and who is also standing in the place usually occupied by a pop/rock idol absolute dynamite. To brush this sort of stuff under the carpet, especially in an oversexed youth culture, is bordering on the ludicrous (to use one of David Beckham's favourite words).

Getting down to the nitty-gritty of discussing pride, ego and sexuality with our young worship leaders of both sexes is absolutely vital. We need to support them as they will be prime targets for spiritual attack, and they need to realise that when they lead they spiritually project a lot of their 'stuff', be that helpful or unhelpful, in their group's direction.

Another issue compounded by lack of integrity in males is the difficulty many girls have with male leadership of any description. This may be due to an abusive or absent father figure, and these sensitivities are unhealthily exacerbated when young men don't walk the talk.

[Connecting]

As a leader, it is essential to relate and connect during a time of gathered worship. You are basically trying to defuse the 'them and us' scenario. I don't believe that this stuff is an optional extra. The moment you throw yourself in front of people, there is a perception that you are different or raised up in some way, and levelling with folks through what you say or do and how you say or do it is key. For me, sometimes this can be as simple as chatting about a funny situation that day, or speaking about a subject close to the hearts of those in the group.

The best recent example of this happened because easyJet had flown me to an event in Belfast, but flown my guitar to Budapest! For six hours or so, I didn't know where my guitar was (constant companion of ten years) and I was absolutely gutted. Just before I stood up to lead worship, I realised that what I had experienced was just a little like losing a child. I shared with everyone that my guts were giving me just a small taste of how intensely God must long for us to 'come home' to him. There was a genuine sense of connection and empathy. (Unbeknown to me, the preacher was speaking on the Prodigal Son.)

As well as letting people see your humanity, you need to show people you know and care where they are coming from. (This is of course presuming that you do care where they are coming from!) You can achieve this verbally or through what you do musically. Whenever we use the riff from 'Lose Yourself' by Eminem as the introduction and groove for the hymn 'Praise my Soul, the King of Heaven' (you have to try it!) an unmistakable connection is made with young people. I bumped into two grungy lads on the street after a worship event and they said, 'The Eminem hymn was cool! That was when we started getting into it.'

For young people, stories are essential to communication. Leading worship is no different. You can stand up at the start of a worship session and speak absolute truth with little effect. The postmodern generation's reaction will be: 'Okay, that may be true. Now what's next?'

Tell the exact same truth as a story and you have a chance of it getting to where it needs to be. A good story creates a context through humour or emotion into which truth can be injected. It is also likely to be more memorable.

The lost guitar story is an example. It is in the nature of a worship leader to want to inspire a group of people with 'reasons why it would be a good idea to sing now'. We earnestly give God the best PR job we can, desperately trying to convince folks to engage. I sometimes worry that there is an ever thinner line of separation between a worship leader and a spin doctor. Inevitably the pre-song statement ends with something like, 'So let's really mean this one and give it everything.' The problem is that in some ways we are mixing two mediums. We are using reason alone to provoke both a rational and emotional response. Stating that 'A+B=C so we should do X' may have worked in the 1970s, but it just doesn't work now. The truth needs to resonate with young people. They need it to 'ring true' or illuminate something of their experience before they will respond. How we communicate has a huge impact on how they respond in worship.

There is no point pretending you are not there to lead. It is best to be strategic, thoughtful and honest about it. God gifts people with communication skills. Don't be ashamed of them. Use them. People will follow your lead further and deeper if empathy has been established.

[Mood Music]

Getting a sense of where God wants to take a session and having an appreciation of where the group is starting from are absolute non-negotiables. The first thing I tell young people who are beginning to lead worship is that it is easy to know where you are, but the challenge is to know where they are. I have experienced too many worship sessions where the feel, rhythm and energy are completely dependent on the mood of the leader. I call them 'Grand Old Duke of York' worship sessions. Up when he/she is up and down when they are down. Don't pretend you are somewhere that you aren't, but leadership of any kind requires seeing the bigger picture beyond your present feelings. Of course, God can use the personal journey he is taking you on to lead the rest of the people, but that is different to imposing all the volatility of human temperament on everyone else. The group may be in need of a time of questioning and soul-searching, while you are bouncing up and down. Or the opposite could also be true.

[Pressure]

We also need to release leaders from the pressure of having to reach the intense 'worship experience' moment the last ten years have defined as the 'correct' climax of sung worship.

I know the temptation only too well, but you just have to hear the dodgy theology we use to describe such moments to realise we may be planting unhelpful subliminal messages. When we say 'At that point, God really showed up' the unspoken message is that we are always at the ballgame, and God only occasionally bothers to turn up. This is more than dangerous, and more likely the opposite of the truth. Of course I'm not saying there aren't times of special blessing when 'the Spirit blows where it wills' and God may lead us into wilderness times, but in general our language in and around these issues needs a serious overhaul. 'And now the worship time...' is a classic. It unwittingly disavows all that has happened previously from being worship.

[Worship Idol]

The dynamics of leadership often shift when young people are confronted by impressive settings and very gifted people. I fear that we could be spiralling down into a culture of celebrity worship leaders. We run the risk of replicating the values of the pop world and mainstream youth culture, rather than subverting them. Anyone selling in the youth market knows the importance of brand association; singling out and elevating characters and celebrities as focal points for mass merchandising. With the best will in the world, it is extremely hard to not create something similar in the ever-growing industry of 'worship music'. There is a worrying suggestion that the good stuff only happens when you are in the hands of experts, and that increasing the size of a gathering increases its significance or depth.

We have been aware of an increasing need to watch this dynamic at Summer Madness (Ireland's Christian youth festival), where the worship leader was increasingly becoming the lightning conductor for all that seemed to be happening. Amazing things were happening in times of sung worship, and the full extent of this was bouncing back to me via email. Even in these emails I started to notice that with the responsibility of leading comes the responsibility of making sure that whenever a connection occurs people fully channel the energy into their relationship with God, and don't dilute it with a desire to be a fan or follower.

An attempt to derail this was the introduction of 'team leading' where two, and then gradually three or four, people were able to lead during a session of worship. This does clash with many innate desires to be able to control things, but is a healthy process for all those involved; learning to work together, to compromise, to learn each other's songs, and to pray for each other. Many folks testified to the importance of the unspoken message this was communicating as one person gave way to another with the mix of older and younger, male and female, guitar and keyboard-driven leadership. Modelling service and cooperation, which is actually much harder work than just running the show yourself, really helped to steer things away from celebrity creation. This same thinking can be applied to leading a small group. It may start off as more work, but in the long run it may be healthier to have two or three folks leading together each week.

[Identifying Worship Leaders]

People often ask me, 'What are the keys to identifying young worship leaders?' They are thinking along the lines of a talent-spotting question, in the same way that Simon Cowell gets asked what he looks for in a Pop Idol. The questioner is expecting thoughts on attitude, leadership, musical ability, etc, which are all absolutely valid.

It can disappoint them when I respond with this story.

I have twice been the 'worship leader' living in the house while being far from the 'leader of worship' in the household. In any situation it is reasonably easy to see who has the biggest desire to connect with God. In the first house, my great friend Tim was the one who unknowingly called us all back to God from the most random situations on the net, in front of the TV, or during a barbecue. 'Leader of worship' also accurately describes how he led us in keeping the house clean and doing the dishes.

My current housemate is Chris, who lifts my soul by unashamedly singing passionate songs to her beloved. Her voice fills the hallways and God is lifted up for me to see. It is a serious blessing to be led like that. People like Tim and Chris inspire me with their lives to give God what he's due 24/7, and I believe that there you have our true worship leaders. They may never touch a musical instrument or spin vinyl, but they inspire us with their passion and consistency. Giving these folks the opportunity to lead sessions of worship is helpful in modelling what worship really is. Those with up-front ability can often be lacking in depth and quality of relationship. It is not hard to look impressively devoted when leading worship. Close your eyes, look to the heavens, sound humble, and you're there. I know because I've done it. But God cares far more about the regularity of my life of worship. The real test of a worshipper is what priority they give to worship when no one is looking. What better way of making it clear that 'worship isn't just music' than having someone whose worship priorities outstrip their musical priorities as team leader. Someone like this can keep everyone's eyes on the bigger picture, and facilitate non-musical avenues and understanding.

[Invisible Leader?]

All the above discussion is based on the assumption that you have any 'leader' at all. With the wide availability of recorded material and visuals for worship, using a DJ or someone less visible may help to rub the raw edge off young people's authority hangups. Sometimes the end product is people being led without realising they are being led. Good leadership leaves people confident in what is going on, but doesn't intrude into the space that postmodern young people crave. For example in a time of silence with prayers displayed on a screen, the person who devised the presentation has very strongly led the group but that may not be the perception amongst the young people.

> *But of a good leader who talks little when his work is*
> *done, his aim fulfilled, they will say: We did it ourselves.'*
>
> *Lao-Tzu*

[Leader versus Facilitator]

Many events now have worship facilitators or curators rather than 'leaders'. Perhaps one person is responsible for facilitating the whole meeting by coordinating everyone else's moments of leadership. Their role is to encourage and empower everyone to make a contribution, and in some way manage the flow of events.

Interaction and involvement are central to the way the New Testament, which often underlines everyone's role in contributing rather than relying on one leader, instructs us to do worship.

> *Speak to one another with psalms, hymns and spiritual*
> *songs.*
>
> *Ephesians 5:19*

Genuine leadership facilitates this, rather than stifling it. Preparation is essential for an open system like this to work otherwise impromptu slots are predictably filled each week by the 'usual suspects', who relegate the introverts and those struggling more with their faith to the role of spectators. These interactive values are at the heart of many of the worship ideas in the final section of this book.

[Qs]

- ◉ Have you identified the real 'leaders of worship' in your group?
- ◉ Have you any non-musical leaders?
- ◉ How much of the leadership truly connects?
- ◉ What jobs could you delegate?

The Wall

One of my most humbling experiences of leading worship came at Spring Harvest in 2002. We had already spent three amazing days with a fantastic group of 11–14-year-olds, and God was moving powerfully. Things had been going so well I told someone it was one of the best weeks of my life, but it all changed on the fourth night.

As soon as we took to the stage I knew something was wrong. A dark feeling began to gnaw at my gut and nothing went right. The band couldn't hear what I was saying or singing. No matter how hard I tried, I couldn't get their attention. The sense of free worship from previous nights had vanished. Everything was muted and I felt alone and vulnerable. I tried a few ideas, said a few things, prayed a few prayers, switched songs – it was like banging my head against a stone wall. We were bedevilled by a constant stream of annoyances such as guitar leads popping out and strings breaking, and the harder we tried the faster we got nowhere.

[Don't underestimate the power of a crew of praying teenagers. Breakthrough and victory aren't dependent on those up front praying, leading or prophesying.]

Then I suddenly realised what I had to do. I had to let go, depend on God, depend on the people around me. Before I really knew what I was saying, I asked everyone to put a hand on the shoulder of the person to their left and their right. I asked them to pray for God the Holy Spirit to flow into them and through them to enable us all to worship. I felt like I couldn't pray at all. What happened next was an awesome explosion of spiritual energy that consumed everything in its path. The volume of singing and noise in the room seemed to multiply by a factor of ten. Most of us in the band were driven to our knees, still playing. The minutes that followed were some of the most honest and broken moments of worship I have ever experienced. God was piercingly holy and blindingly bright. People were crying with joy because they had met face to face with a powerful yet loving God.

But God wasn't finished with me. An 11-year-old lad came up to me at the end of the evening and asked if he could pray for me. 'Andy, I could see what was going on tonight,' he said.

Wow, he's pretty perceptive, I thought to myself, I didn't think I had let my frustration show. 'Ah, the strings, the PA and stuff,' I said.

'No, no, I mean I saw what was happening. You and the band were playing your instruments and marching towards this massive big wall, but there were arrows coming at you from all sides. Because you were at the front, Andy, loads of them were scoring direct hits on you. You kept trying to move forward, but you couldn't. The wall was blocking you, and no matter how hard you tried it would not budge. Then everybody prayed, and there was an explosion that just ripped through the wall. Together we then moved through to the other side, and it was great there.'

I just lost it. An 11-year-old had seen precisely in the Spirit what I had failed to see. The words 'and it was great there' reverberated in my head for hours after. The innocent had summed up in a simple expression what I long for young people to experience in worship.

I had learned a really important lesson. The spiritual ability of 11–14-year-olds to lead me out of the darkness was humbling. Don't underestimate the power of a crew of praying teenagers. Breakthrough and victory aren't dependent on those up front praying, leading or prophesying. Let's raise up an army that marches on its knees.

Chapter 5

Me and Do, Do and Me

When people look back at the late 20th and early 21st centuries, will they look at our frantic activity and marvel at our efficiency? Or will they weep at the broken relationships that act as buffers as we bounce from one task to the next? Will they say we were awfully good at 'how' but never bothered to find out 'why'? Will they wipe their brows and say, 'Phew! I'm glad I wasn't born until after the great emotional crash of 2014.'

Humanity's ability to stop and reflect is shrinking by the day. We are so preoccupied by our thoughts and agendas that truly experiencing anything without interrupting ourselves is becoming more and more difficult.

Why have we become like this?

> With our own agenda firmly in the forefront of our thinking it is easy for self-interest to superimpose false imaginings on the true picture of God.

Many young people struggle to love, or even like, themselves but that doesn't stop them being obsessed with themselves. It is the '80s legacy of individualism, though egoism was in vogue for a millennium or two before. We start each day by crafting a to-do list mostly designed to serve ourselves. Our devotion to sorting our stuff out or getting things done often leaves us no room to be aware of what other people need.

When Descartes was searching for a definite starting point for his philosophy, he doubted the reality of everything until he came to a reality he could not doubt: 'I think, therefore I am!' From his point of view, the only thing I can be sure of, what I truly know is real, is myself. This helps explain why we often stay locked inside our own heads. If my own thoughts are the only thoughts I experience then, as Ronald Rolheiser puts it in his book *The Shattered Lantern*, 'My heartaches, my headaches, my wounds, my problems, my worries are real. Other people's lives and the larger community and its concerns are not as real!' We instinctively invest our time in what we believe to be most real, and that happens to be us. How does this preoccupation interact with worship?

The north coast of Northern Ireland is probably one of my favourite parts of the whole world. On holiday there one year my capability to fully appreciate its crashing waves and jutting headlands was seriously diminished by my preoccupation with the theft a day earlier of about £500 from our CD stall at a gig. I don't think it would have made much difference to me whether I was in the slums of Bangladesh or the hanging gardens of Babylon – the greens were greyed, the sounds were muted and the clouds were darkened.

> When efficiency becomes an end in itself we buy the promise that it will improve our lives, creating more time for what we really want to do.

Nothing had changed the reality of what lay before me. The beach had not shortened. The cliffs had not shrunk. The sea had not been polluted. What had changed was me. The same applies to the reality of God in worship. Yes, we must bring all our frustrations and dilemmas to him; but if we are truly preoccupied, as we tend to be, are we experiencing God as he really is? Or do we see a version tainted by our current foibles and mindset? We may miss something of his beauty. With our own agenda firmly in the forefront of our thinking it is easy for self-interest to superimpose false imaginings of his character on the true picture of God.

I believe the more we encourage young people to stop and take in the scenery, the more they will develop an awareness of the one true God. Young people have difficulty transcending awareness of self, but activities that encourage them to take time and focus on the true character of God can develop discipline that crosses over into corporate and personal worship times. Quoting Rolheiser again, 'We are a generation scared of silence in the same way that we are scared of death.' This is not a coincidence. Our activist minds know the truth – when we die, we cannot do any more. 'The soul does not fear death, but the ego is scared stiff of it.'

[Restlessness]

When I sit down, within a second my brain is bombarding itself with one hundred and one tasks I could be completing instead of stopping for ten minutes to read or think. I was alerted to this when buzzing around the UK leading Youth For Christ's band, TVB. Our lives were dominated by schedules and journeys. It was only in the years after coming off the road that I noticed what it had done to me. It is the little things that really freak me out. Perhaps you can identify with them. When I am making toast I rush to get the bread in the toaster first as I know it will give me a good 90 seconds to do something profitable, whether it is slicing cheese or hunting for a tin of tuna! As I enter my room, the first thing I do is boot up my computer as I know that in the minute or so it takes to get going I will be able to tidy up some clothes, find my lost keys (wishful thinking) and write a song or two.

It is a disease. When efficiency becomes an end in itself we buy the promise that it will improve our lives, creating more time for what we really want to do, but instead we find more things to fit into the extra time. Consider the array of gadgets on sale for saving time and effort. I remember smiling at the irony of it as a frustrated young man beside me on a crowded train attempted to get his pocket PC internet chatroom program working. Obviously the rest of us in the carriage weren't human enough to communicate with.

For me, the story of Mary and Martha provides the perfect antidote to all our restlessness and preoccupation.

> As Jesus and his disciples were on their way, he came to a village where a woman named Martha opened her home to him. She had a sister called Mary, who sat at the Lord's feet listening to what he said. But Martha was distracted by all the preparations that had to be made. She came to him and asked, "Lord, don't you care that my sister has left me to do the work by myself? Tell her to help me!"
>
> "Martha, Martha," the Lord answered, "you are worried and upset about many things, but only one thing is

needed. Mary has chosen what is better, and it will not be taken away from her."

Luke 10:38–42

I find this one of the most challenging passages in the New Testament because I identify very strongly with Martha. Whether it is the efficiency of your mobile for text messages or the speed of your broadband connection, everything is pointing us towards (and praising increases in) productivity so we have more time to cram in more entertainment or work. I believe it is vital to foster in young people the importance of silence and reflection before their lives are swallowed, as they will be, by pressing deadlines and schedules. But to do this the values of a whole culture need to be turned on their head, and that is exactly what Jesus does by saying 'only one thing is needed'. In the midst of their juggling exams, sports, website design and part-time jobs, it's releasing for young people to know that only one thing is needed. Now that is a great theme for a worship session.

[It is our duty to prevent the next generation inheriting our restlessness, preoccupation and obsessive functionality.]

[Facilitating Silence]

Silence is a pretty large pain barrier for young people to go through, but it is worth persisting even if it feels like it 'didn't work' the first time. Images, random words or Bible verses looping on a screen can be helpful in focusing minds that are prone to wandering. Everything in you will be screaming 'make it stop! – I can't cope with this any longer!', but you need to hold out, bite your tongue and pray hard. One effective way we have found of doing this is to warn folks that when they arrive that night they will be asked to be silent. Then we arrive early to prepare the room with visuals, cushions, tea lights etc. Have yourself and the team already silent before anyone arrives, otherwise the volume is set at 'mumble level' and no one has the confidence to enjoy actually being silent. You should post a 'bouncer' on the door to politely remind everyone that all phones need to be switched off, and that all talking needs to be finished before entry. An announcement or the visuals should give some lead as to how long everyone will remain silent for, again so that people are not left wondering 'What is going on?' or 'And how long will this last?' If you honestly feel that some further leadership is needed, then try speaking just one word every couple of minutes. You could list the fruits of the spirit from Galatians 5.

Encouraging silence is obviously a great way to slow ourselves down, but we must be careful that activities like this don't become another thing we just do. Restfulness has almost been privatised into another activity. 'Yes, I better schedule in some restfulness for next week.' When we think restful, we think chilling out in a sauna or lying on a beach. Real restfulness is more a way of life than another activity. It is a contentment with the ordinariness of life, running counter to the culture's greed for experience.

I believe that how we craft worship experiences can have a profound effect on these issues. Will we build in to programs the space to reflect, the space to listen and the space to be affirmed for just being?

It is our duty to prevent the next generation inheriting our restlessness, preoccupation and obsessive functionality. Their habits in prayer and worship are programmed in these formative years, and as I know only too well it is extremely hard to rewrite the program.

[Qs]
- When was the last time you truly 'stopped' for an hour?
- What is preventing your young people from 'stopping'?
- In what ways could you facilitate young people 'stopping'?

Chapter 6

Reverence

How do you explore reverence with a generation that doesn't think twice about answering their mobile if it rings during worship? How can you model it when the leader also has her phone on, sneakily leaving it in vibrate mode? Perhaps we have been guilty of neglecting the 'reverence' aspect of our worship in recent years, so it's not surprising the next generation is taking it to the next level.

Ask any teacher or parent what they see as the primary problem of this generation. Many will shake their weary heads and say, 'Lack of respect!' They go on, 'You should hear the abuse I have to put up with' or 'Much more of this and society will fall apart.' In an age when young people are disinclined to show any respect to people that they can see, it's a huge challenge to encourage them to respect a God they cannot see. And respect is only a stepping stone towards reverence and awe.

> Say you're in contact with God and you 'hang up' for something else that comes along, what are you saying? How does it make God feel?

Obviously reverence is something that comes from deep within, and therefore we should never measure someone's reverence by the yardstick of behaviour we regard as appropriate. I'm reminded of the challenge laid before us when we pray for folks to become Christians – are we praying for them to become more like Jesus or to become nicer so our lives are simpler. Young people may act in ways we regard as inappropriate, but sometimes at the root this is more to do with the 'rules of engagement' they have learnt from their family and school than with a lack of reverence for God.

Some might say, as I have already, that reverence is something that can only be caught, not taught. On Mount Sinai, Moses didn't hear a talk telling him to fear God. He was left in no doubt as to the proper attitude when they met face to face. Encouragingly, this attitude did begin to rub off on the Israelites as they saw how Moses' face was shining. Perhaps much of the responsibility lies with us as we model reverence for an awesome God not just during 'worship time' but as we prepare for and disengage from such times.

We've had some success using simple role play scenarios to get folks thinking about what is going on in worship situations.

You're on the phone to your best mate (on their home phone) when their mobile rings. They say 'gotta go', hang up on you and answer the other call without explanation. How do you feel? What made them decide to take the call?

> Take the intensity of staring into someone's eyes and multiply that by ten thousand and you begin to know the depth of love that the ultimate lover has for us. We may break off the gaze, but he never will.

Say you're in contact with God and you 'hang up' for something else that comes along, what are you saying? How does it make God feel? How did you decide who to be in communication with? Folks don't often spot that they are making value judgements.

Another angle on this is that many of the young people I know only respect people who are 'hard'. Might part of their lack of respect for God be that we haven't shown them the full extent of God's character? Have they been mis-sold 'gentle Jesus, meek and mild' by our nativity plays and Sunday School stories? What about the revolutionary who literally 'turned the tables' on the establishment? That kind of behaviour definitely generates some respect.

This issue is also a great example of our theology being moulded by the songs we sing. If a goodly proportion of our songs speak about an awesome holy God, in a way that is God-focused and not me-focused, then there is more of a chance of that reality filtering through to our understanding and behaviour. However, if these sorts of songs are vastly outnumbered by songs that focus on us and our relationship to Jesus as a lover and friend, then thoughts of awe are likely to be less prevalent than thoughts of love.

One very helpful way of explaining these two sides of one coin is through the word used most commonly in the New Testament for 'worship'.

[Proskuneo]

The Greek word *proskuneo*, which literally means 'to come toward and kiss', is used 59 times in the New Testament, while all the other words for 'worship' are in single figures. It beautifully sums up the dual intimacy and reverence of worship with the image of someone stooping to kiss a hand but maintaining eye contact. Visibly there is stooping, revealing the invisible attitudes of reverence and respect. There is also a connection via the eyes – the doorway to the soul. Eye contact can communicate love and awe, but being so intimate it can be uncomfortable when mutual trust is lacking or a relationship is out of sync. This is why we struggle in times of intimate worship when we have not confessed our sins to God, or we are being intentionally rebellious in some area of our lives.

> Have we presented God as so rational and so defined that people have ceased to fear him? Have we ceased to respect his awesome power because we do not tell stories of it or see it in action?

Take the intensity of staring into someone's eyes and multiply that by ten thousand and you begin to know the depth of love that the ultimate lover has for us. We may break off the gaze, but he never will. Unlike earthly lovers, however, we look upwards into those eyes because we are bowed low in the presence of one so great who is endowed with royal majesty. We don't have too many contexts for stooping or kneeling these days unless you get an OBE or a knighthood, so you may have to explain some context. Lastly we place a kiss on the hand. Intimacy and reverence come together spectacularly in this moment. The fact that the kiss is on the hand helpfully distinguishes it from purely romantic love for young people. Interestingly we are initiating a forward action by our choice, but only in response to the outstretched hand proffered graciously. So much truth is being conveyed. This word *proskuneo* is just phenomenal. This God is just phenomenal.

Here's a simple idea – before a sung worship time get everyone into pairs. Explain the meaning of the word and illustrate it with some willing volunteers. Get the pairs to try it themselves, both as giver and recipient of the kiss. Ask for comments as to how this felt, and what they noticed. Usual comments are, 'It's a two-way thing', 'I had to swallow my pride to stoop down', 'There was respect', 'It felt close'. During the sung worship time remind everyone of what they had been doing and let it inform their posture, attitude, and language to God in worship.

The success of this exercise does depend somewhat on the maturity of your group, but if everyone can get over their initial giggles it is an effective way of planting in their heads a correct attitude to worship.

[Spirituality]

One of the most encouraging things about this generation is their thirst for things that are beyond this world. Unfortunately the postmodern doctrine of pragmatism, which does not question the ethics or morals of any scenario, is applied to all manner of spiritual situations. Whether it is young white witches casting 'good' spells, Derren Brown playing quasi-spiritual mind games, astrologers giving them relationship advice or Colin Fry trying to contact their dead grandmother, all young people care about is whether or not it works. Through mass media like the internet, previously minority information is at your fingertips and who is to say the content of one website is less true than the other 100 million. I shall never forget being in a woman's home when she discovered that her daughter had been downloading spells from a coven website. This generation feels let down by the promise that improved technology will make our lives better. They realise that length, breadth and height are not the only dimensions to be explored.

So here arises an interesting conundrum. It would seem that 'fear of God' (dictionary definition – 'respectful dread') has not actually left our society but has been translocated into the world of spiritists, mediums and vampire-slayers. There can be respectful dread for that stuff all right. Have we presented God as so rational and so defined that people have ceased to fear him? Have we ceased to respect his awesome power because we do not tell stories of it or see it in action? Have we desired to make him so palatable that there is nothing to be afraid of any more?

13 Minutes

Sometimes the hardest thing to develop in young leaders is the confidence and authority to say nothing at all. It has taken me a long time to be able to step into even a little bit of this. If I was leading worship and a silence lasted for more than a minute, I would start squirming. I would worry about what the people in charge were thinking, and listen out for that 'fidgeting' that is the first sign of people getting bored. My desire to provide a 'proper end' and please people was stronger than my desire to do what God wanted.

Then in 2002 I had an experience where I just could not interrupt the silence. I had no choice. God had presenced himself majestically during a time of worship and we ended with everyone repeating 'Holy is the Lord God Almighty'. To have said even one word would have distracted from what he was doing. The only appropriate response was to sink to my knees, and the crowd followed. We spent precious time together and alone with God. Not a sound was heard throughout the massive auditorium. It wasn't until I received a minidisc recording of the evening that I realised the silence had lasted for a full 13 minutes. It had gone by in a second.

> [It is great if young leaders don't need that nervous sideways glance every couple of minutes.]

As I came off the stage, the guy in charge turned to me and said, 'I thought the stage was going to crack in two.' He was referring to what had happened in Tommy Tenney's church (from the book *God Chasers*). Afterwards tears of thanks just kept flowing. God broke something in me that night, and used that to break a barrier in others too. The sound engineer grabbed me and prophesied that same thing.

Lord, help us give you the space to be God.

It won't always be right to leave long periods of silence. That is not my point. My point is that for our young people to have the authority and confidence to stick their necks out (and leaving silence is one of the best examples of this) we need to let them know that we trust them to lead. And when I say lead I mean really lead, not just pretend to lead, being in effect a mouthpiece for the person in the shadows who is pulling the strings. It is great if young leaders don't need that nervous sideways glance every couple of minutes.

We must not only release them to be leaders, but also release them to be worshippers. If they are thinking about leadership to the extent that their worship is being inhibited, it is unlikely that their worship will lead other people's worship. At times they need to know that it is all right to simply do what they would do if there was no one else in the room.

Chapter 7

Words and Pictures

When David wrote a psalm or when Jesus spoke to a first-century crowd, they used scenes, imagery and motifs from their own time and context. Today's younger generation learns, loves and breathes by means of illustration, but there seems to be a barrier with regard to modern imagery and language in worship songs. We appear to have created a new language and culture that is worship, and sanitised them so that real words like 'metal' and 'phone' are out of place in songs. Don't we add to the problems young people face when we split their lives artificially into God-stuff and world-stuff? It never ceases to amaze me how some of the young people I know switch between two completely different but believable guises; church person and school person. Each persona says exactly the right things for the circumstances. (There are plenty of us adults who do that too, mind you.)

> Does a young person in 2004 know what a refining fire is? Not that we should ditch this rich biblical imagery, but let's stretch our minds to add more accessible pictures and language.

John Bell of the Iona Community speaks much of the need to sing about 'God in the kitchen', because if he's not real there can he truly be real anywhere? Granted there are some constraints on our language, because of our desire to use it poetically, but surely our primary problem is an horrendous urge to play it safe in our worship vocabulary. Perhaps this is what makes our Christianity seem more impressive when we're at a big gathering. The language of our songs is the language of the church gathered. We are unimpressive as the church dispersed, because our lexicon of worship does not stretch to playgrounds, classrooms, traffic jams and board meetings. Honestly, we believe what we sing. The words that reverberate in our heads and hearts become our theology, and if words of the real world and its imagery are not taking root then we will stay 'Christian bubble Christians' forever.

Many of today's young people have a vague grasp on the agricultural imagery of ploughing or seed sowing, but it's not enough for them to get inside the image and experience its power. Does a young person in 2004 know what a refining fire is? Not that we should ditch this rich biblical imagery, but let's stretch our minds to add more accessible pictures and language. Only when you understand a subject can you fully enter into the layers of its imagery, as the following example shows.

[Count the Pennies Dropping]

It was a shock to find out that when Rod Stewart sang 'If I said you had a beautiful body, would you hold it against me?' it wasn't just a reference to taking umbrage for inappropriate comments. In a similar vein, I was admiring the view at a reservoir near Heathrow Airport when I realised that I could see Windsor Castle in the distance. I got quite excited, and as its silhouette shimmered in the late summer haze I could make out the Royal Standard flapping limply at the top of the flagpole. I turned to my American picnic companion and said knowledgeably, 'You know, that means the queen is in residence! That means she's like, just over there!' In the midst of my excitement, I had a sudden realisation that I had sung about this many, many times.

There's a flag flying high from the castle of my heart, for the king is in residence there!

For years I had manfully sung this Sunday School classic as loud as I could to impress all around, and swung my arms around in suitable flag-waving and castle-forming actions. But now I panicked as I realised that for all of that time I hadn't had a blind clue as to the significance of what I was singing. Sure we had a great communal experience, and felt like we belonged to something, but had we missed the boat completely? For it to be helpful, we need imagery we can understand. It got me thinking about all the other songs I sang as I was growing up, and it was worrying to realise how many I had happily sung in complete ignorance.

As a polite young church boy, I didn't really mind, but someone coming from outside the church in this age of short attention spans may well mind to the extent that they disengage. So you can see why I am so passionate that we don't fall into this trap again, lulled by the positive experience we are creating, unaware that in a generation's time our young people may wake up with a jolt like I did saying, 'Did you feel the mountains tremble? What was that all about?'

[New Image?]

We have been using a song that likens our relationship with God to a mobile phone connection. Certain words seem awkward and out of place the first time through, but the fact that young people know everything there is to know about the world of mobile phones means that they are truly entering into the imagery being used. e.g. constant 4 bars out of 4 reception between God and us, the fact that he is never engaged, that the relationship needs regular charging, etc. Those thoughts resonate with their everyday lives. Until Jacob described God as a shepherd in Genesis 48, the chances are that no one else had spoken of him in those terms. Every metaphor or simile was new once.

One of the most significant songs we have been using with young people in the last few years has been 'Help Me Hold On'.

The words of the chorus are:

Help me hold on to things that will last
Help me learn from mistakes in my past
Take the rubbish that's filling my life
Fill me up with only you.

In many contexts young people have latched onto the simple concept of stashing what is useful and good, and trashing what needs to be gone from their lives. The song also provides plenty of scope for meaningful physical activity with bins and boxes. However in discussion with someone about recording the song, the suggestion was made that the word 'rubbish' should be replaced because it didn't sit right. In the end we pushed through the pain barrier and didn't change anything, but it is a good example of the mental battles we have to fight to escape our 'worship culture' box.

This escape will probably have to occur at grassroots level, because it's unlikely to be led by the worship industry. I'm not laying blame here because it's simply that profit margins in the Christian trade are not large enough to enable lots of experimentation. You may think it a strange thing to mention, but much of what happens at a local level is strongly steered, intentionally or unintentionally, by the wider market. To ignore this fact is to keep one's head in the sand. What works on a large scale at an event or festival may not work in a local setting.

[
Of course the use of romantic imagery is not wrong, as our God is a jealous lover who woos us and entreats us to return to our first love, but our current societal context means that we must be wise to the power at play.
]

The other danger of this middle ground, mass-marketed method of song distribution is that we are restricted to songs using certain forms of acceptable words, and so only certain experiences are carried in worship. The question is how does this impact young people? Does it lull them into being receptive consumerist sponges, or spark them into being creative, thinking individuals who bring the reality of their lives before God.

[Fish]

When Jesus spoke in parables it was revolutionary, but it wasn't rocket science. He just had the best ever human eyes to see the gospel in action in the ordinariness of seed-sowing and travelling. We need to ask for his eyes, to see pictures of the kingdom of God in the kitchen, the living room and on the street.

In Luke 5:10 Jesus plants a ticking time-bomb in the fishermen's heads and hearts – 'Don't be afraid; from now on you will catch men.' Would this statement have had the same impact on Simon and his companions if it had not referred directly to the activity of their daily life? It created a context for what was about to occur. Whenever they touched a net or a sail, there would have been a resonance with this moment. A young person today is highly unlikely to have an in-depth knowledge of the fishing trade that will provide a similar resonance and understanding of what it is to be involved in evangelism. Likening our activities to attracting new players to a team or new customers to a brand may seem outlandish or just not accurate enough, but I suspect that likening the extension of the kingdom to one of the poorest trades on earth raised an eyebrow or two in Jesus' day. So let's experiment a little, in the knowledge that no picture will ever be perfect.

[DIY Liturgy]

One useful challenge is to create some modern liturgy, which is often a less painful way of introducing contemporary language. Words without an 'attached' melody (even though you may want to use an ambient track to support the spoken words) are free of the constraints of lyricism and the desperate need to rhyme with refrigerator. It might be worth considering a regular liturgy that your group co-authors to give it as wide an ownership as possible. The process of creating the structure and content of the liturgy is a fantastic team-building and priority-exposing exercise. It causes folks to think about exactly what they believe, and in times where all focus shifts onto one aspect of God's character it will provide a balance and a reassuring but always challenging familiarity – as do various ancient liturgies.

Workshop style sessions often prove useful here, with particular parts of the group working on specific sections of the text. Usually many questions are needed to draw people's natural creativity out of them and reinforce the concept of what you are trying to do. For example: 'So you want to say that God is strong... When do you need someone strong in your life? You could just take the easy route out and talk about our strong tower, but I certainly haven't had to run up one to get away from any marauding Vikings recently. In 2004, needing strength makes me think bodyguard.'

Often a way of kick-starting this process is by suggesting a first line, from which the rest can follow. e.g.

We can't imagine why you love us...

God. Listing your qualities would fill a newspaper...

Two of the areas where we need to be aware of current cultural baggage are romance and majesty.

[Romance]

When combined with music, romantic words take on a poetry that can be very persuasive and have massive power over this love-deprived generation. Of course the use of romantic imagery is not wrong, as our God is a jealous lover who woos us and entreats us to return to our first love, but our current societal context means that we must be wise to the power at play.

The majority of songs young people write at song writing workshops have at their core this valid, but narrow, method of communicating with God. They are representative of a desire for fast-track intimacy that is reflected from the writer's actual relationships. Sam Hargreaves, a final year student at London School of Theology, decided to investigate the frequency of romantic imagery and language in an array of modern worship songs and was so surprised at the extent of what he found that he titled his dissertation 'Jesus is my Girlfriend'.

> The tabloid press has made us feel that we own the royal family rather than them ruling us, so it is not surprising that young people struggle to fully appreciate the privilege that it is to come before a king.

We must understand the average young person's concept of romantic love. Without a moral framework of any sort, they download the values and practices of romantic love unfiltered through the mass media of soap opera relationships and celebrity hook-ups. The blaring but unspoken messages that are communicated, and end up accepted as truth, are:

- a partner is just another consumer commodity, primarily for improving your standard of life, and when they cease to do that they are as expendable as anything else we have attained or purchased. And therefore;
- love itself is a conditional, time-limited thing that has more to do with feelings than choice.

Many young people also have experiences of hurt from relationships. It is not hard to see why so many can engage intensely in intimate moments of worship and then a few months later, or at times even hours later, can be a million miles away from someone who loves them unconditionally. If we reduce worship to just another 'love fix' we are in dangerous territory. The problem is that the world's interpretation of love is projected onto the love of God as described in a lyric. Combine that with the right sort of music and someone might gradually get the wrong idea.

I would advise simply checking that in any given session there is a balance between songs with romantic language and more objective proclamatory songs. The greatest disaster would be if we threw the baby out with the bathwater, discarding the beautiful songs of intimacy that have been written in the last fifteen years or so.

[Majesty]

I suspect that we have lost something of the awe inherent in the statement that God is king.

To this generation of young Britons, the monarch has always been female, benevolent and limited to 'virtual' power rather than political clout. When someone from the Middle Ages addressed God as 'King of kings' or said 'You are my King', I reckon that they had a decidedly different slant on what it actually meant.

In those days, the king or queen engendered loyalty, support and fear. Their power was ultimate and God-given, and it was distributed how they saw fit. There were no juries or parliaments to consult before uttering the words, 'Off with his head'. Has our understanding of the power and majesty of God been dimmed as the power of the monarch has been diluted?

The tabloid press has made us feel that we own the royal family rather than them ruling us, so it is not surprising that young people struggle to fully appreciate the privilege that it is to come before a king. The Windsor family's proximity through the press makes dignity and grandeur rather difficult concepts.

I will never forget visiting Hampton Court Palace last year. To get to the Throne Room we had to go through many outer rooms, during which time if we had been attempting to visit the sovereign we would have been vetted by many courtiers. But nothing compared to what awaited us in the Guard Room, where the sovereign's armed guards would have resided. There are still 3,000 functional weapons hung on the walls of that room. I wouldn't fancy my chances! Add to that intense level of security the sheer beauty and majesty of the building, its gardens and its setting, and for the first time I was beginning to get a sense of what it truly meant to say that Jesus is King of kings, i.e. that he is quite literally the King to top all kings. If an earthly king resides in such splendour, how much more glorious is our heavenly King. How much more does he deserve a bended knee, he who gave up that splendour to become a human baby.

It is also worth underlining the privilege that we now have because of Jesus' death. In previous times if you entered the Throne Room and the king did not want to see you, the offence was punishable by death. The difference is stark. Compare this with Hebrews 4:16:

> *Let us then approach the throne of grace with confidence,*
> *so that we may receive mercy and find grace to help us in*
> *our time of need.*

We have lost the sense of privilege in these verses that would have been obvious to the medieval reader, who would not have dreamt of coming near an earthly king never mind a heavenly one.

We have made some progress on this front through telling stories and recreating throne rooms from gazebos! Royalty-associated images on screen will help, along with the famous MP3 of Pastor Loughridge 'He's my King! He's indescribable', available on the web at www.youthwork.co.uk/resources/. The song 'King of Kings, Majesty' also helps the unpacking process.

[Qs]

◉ How could we encourage young songwriters to use modern language and imagery?

In the next chapter, we move onto another subject where the associations of the language we use are of primary importance – family.

Chapter 8

Family

Family is a tough area. I will never forget the afternoon when a youth worker friend of mine came back to my house after a school lunchtime club. The young people had all been asked to fill in a questionnaire as part of joining the club. On flicking through the sheets, what jumped out at him was that only seven of the 31 young people came from what is called a nuclear family. My mind wandered to a chilling, though doubtless inaccurate, irony. What is an alternative to nuclear weapons? Conventional weapons. I guess the depressing conclusion is that the other 24 young people came from 'conventional' families. When I meet young people whose lives are scarred or stifled by this new convention, I get sad and mad. I know that often these situations arise through no fault of the parents involved, and also that some of the most impressive young people I've known have grown up in single-parent families, but an awareness of this massively changing demographic is a vital tool in crafting worship language and experiences.

> [Speaking truth during worship is incredibly powerful.]
> Never be afraid to speak what you know to be the truth.

How we view God and interact with him is often inextricably linked to how we view our family relationships, and vice versa. Many songs are full of the language of interrelation and family, whether in the description of the members of the Trinity or with reference to us. It is so easy for a young person to read these words with a 'family filter' in front of their eyes.

I am extremely proud to live in Luton. I really love the place and its people. I know the struggles that many of its young people face. Week by week I meet folk for whom expressing love to someone called 'father' is going to be either a painful or a numb experience. Many young people identify more positively with the mothering aspect of God's nature, as they associate motherhood with more reliability than fatherhood. I'm not suggesting that we make wholesale changes in the language we use in addressing God, but that we need to be aware of the mental and emotional processing young people often have to do so we are able to intelligently help them through it.

[Watch this Space]

Last Easter tears flowed pretty consistently. This subject of family is burning in me and is the key theme of my album *SON*. A lovely lady and her daughter came to speak to me the day after an event where I had used a song called 'Watch this Space'. Before I tell you about them, let me explain the background to the song.

I met a quality 14-year-old called Tim in Manchester a couple of years ago while I was spending some time with his youth group. He was a really lovely lad, but something about the way he was interacting with me and with his mates made me think there were things ticking away below the surface that I didn't know about. Later I found out that his dad hadn't been around since Tim was six. He might have sent birthday cards and turned up at 'appropriate' moments, but he was never around when Tim really wanted to simply share time with him. I could see the gaping hole that had been left in Tim's psyche. It really got to me, as it always does, but this time I put pen to paper and found myself identifying with his situation, attempting to articulate everything that I sensed he was feeling.

I always sang the song with some degree of nervousness, aware that I might not be truthfully representing his thoughts on the matter, but an awesome thing happened. Tim heard me playing his song at Festival Manchester. We were able to chat after the gig, and I apprehensively asked him what he thought of the song. 'Man', he said. 'It said everything I've always wanted to say, but never been able to let out.' It was a special moment, and one which I will never forget. Tim felt someone truly understood where he was coming from, and the song had actually helped him verbalise some stuff for the first time. Awesome. God is very good.

Anyway, back to the lady and her daughter. They were standing arm in arm.

'We just wanted to say that we really felt included last night. No one ever talks about that sort of stuff, and the fact that someone acknowledged it was brilliant,' they said, and I shall never forget the mutual look of love that passed from mother to daughter. 'We've been on our own for five or six years now, haven't we, love? But we do good, don't we? We love God and we love each other.'

Cue two more fantastic smiles and a big squeeze. I wasn't holding it together at this point, as you might guess. If ever I needed reminding that I constantly need reminding of where people may be coming from, this was it. Through what I had said from the stage, a connection had somehow been made and it had unlocked a door that let God come streaming through. Let's keep an eye out for these essential keys.

[Prodigal]

We have seen God work powerfully in this area through the story of the Prodigal Son. It actually redeems the word 'father' for some people, as evidenced by many emails in the last few years. The technicolor reality of the character of the prodigal's father seems to displace some of the projection that normally occurs from people's earthly fathers onto their heavenly father. This kind of projection can hamstring young people, as they are acutely sensitive to the negative effects of parental words and attitudes.

The moments where this has occurred most directly have been during a song called 'Open Arms', where the singer is invited to identify with first the younger brother and then the older brother from the story. This 'stepping into the story' seems to help people experience the truth of God's unconditional welcome home without some of the baggage that they might normally bring to the moment. As they realise that this amazing man running towards them is a father, and in fact is representative of the perfect Father, something very biblical, spiritual and wonderful seems to happen. I will never forget the words of a young guy who reported that it was the first time he had let God hold him as a father.

Here is part of an amazing email from someone who also had that experience. She had been walking away from God for quite some time.

When 'Open Arms' came on, I sat up. Something just clicked. I put the song back to the beginning and told Colin to listen to the first verse. That was the stage I was at, and hadn't been able to explain to him. It was this verse that made me realise how I had to go on. I then and

*there sat and out aloud asked God to allow me back into
his arms and to share my every day with me. I know that
I could not have done this without hearing this song, as it
made me realise that God will help anyone that will ask
for it.*

*I know that I have a long way to go, and that this is just
the beginning, but everyone has to begin somewhere, and
here is where I started.*

The words she had been listening to were these.

*I will return to you and say
I am not fit to be your slave
For I have sinned and turned away
My journey home is filled with fear
Of what I'll find when I draw near
Is there a welcome for me here?*

I'm excited that more and more young people are discovering
despite what has been ground into them from early childhood, that
the answer to the question in the last line is 'yes!'

Presenting worship as an unrestrained party of the returning son
clearly resonates with young people on one level. They know what
a party is. They know that there is music, laughter and a carefree
attitude. They also know that parties are best when there is a reason
for them, and I can think of no better reason than the fact that
they are loved unconditionally. The free, over-the-top, celebratory
provision of the as-much-as-you-can-eat party is an earthly echo
of the heavenly love that doesn't expect anything in return.

[Forsaken]

It has also proved useful for some young people to have unpacked
the father-son relationship from the New Testament, illustrating
the depth of love and trust involved, and also the pain of separation
at the time of Jesus' death. Remember those amazing words Jesus
quoted from Psalm 22, 'My God, my God, why have you forsaken
me?' He was not reciting lines in a complex play within a play,
whereby the tragic words are spoken but later the actors return to
normality. He was actually forsaken. Much as it broke God's heart,

the Father was actually cutting himself off from the Son. For the first and last time the very centre of the universe, the Trinity, was being torn apart. Jesus knew what it was to have someone he loved turn their back on him in a moment of need, and incredibly that someone was his Father. He knows their pain.

[Adoption]

Another way of explaining God's fatherhood that seems to release people in worship is the fact that we are adopted children in his family. It is an especially helpful contrast for those who negatively associate God with their natural fathers.

The simple truth is that as the Father's adopted children we have been chosen. In the same way that a husband and wife looking to adopt will select a child, the Father has selected us. We have been specifically and deliberately brought under his authority and care. It is not an accident that we are with him. In a holy inversion of the most hurtful thing that any child hears, he will never regret the day he set eyes on us because that was the day he willingly, without any coercion, made us his own. It is in fact the complete opposite of what many young people experience with their natural fathers.

A lot of children draw the conclusion (rightly or wrongly) that they were an accident or a mistake. They are dumped, left pondering why when voluntary decision-making did become involved the decision was made to leave them. You can see why knowing the truth of their heavenly Father's voluntary selection can be so powerful in helping young people separate their perceptions of true fatherhood from any negative attachments they may have.

Sometimes these attachments are 'front and centre' in a young person's consciousness due to their immediacy. But sometimes they are dormant, remnants of barely remembered times which nevertheless feed automatic assumptions about fatherhood and trust. Often these feelings remain in the dark, unaddressed until an emotional crisis of one kind or another tosses all of them out into the light.

Speaking truth during worship is incredibly powerful. Never be afraid to speak what you know to be the truth. Hearing the truth that Jesus speaks – 'You are chosen, you are mine, you are precious' – is often the trigger to release someone into a new ability to appreciate his love and to know who they really are. Getting your young people to speak truth over each other in the context of worship multiplies this impact. We have facilitated this process by providing 'cue cards' of truths cycling through on a PowerPoint presentation in the background. This is also available on www. youthwork.co.uk/resources/.

[Generation Gap]

One day my friend Jude Smith and I had been chatting over the reasons why young people find it hard to connect with God as a father. We had covered the ground mentioned above, but felt there was something we were missing. A couple of days later Jude sent me an email that cut me to the core. I believe we have been guilty of modelling another stumbling block to this generation.

Basically, do we treat God more as a grandfather than a father? If we analyse the method, frequency and quality of our interaction with him does it add up to a relationship spanning one generation or two? Do we just call in to visit once or twice a week, when it's convenient for our schedule? Do we sit and chat, keeping one eye on the clock, ready to escape to our next important duty? Do we open up and tell the whole truth, or just give edited highlights? Do we really do the hard work of living with someone, like you live with a parent? Intimacy is hard work.

How we relate to God has a major influence on how we perceive him, so it shouldn't surprise us that folks find the 'father thing' hard to grab when we seem to be modelling something else altogether. We want the emotional security of a benevolent grandparent and so that's what we turn God into. We are glad that God is there, but we are happy to leave him at arm's length. His only duties are to give us presents every so often and come to our aid. But to know the full benefits of a father we must know his discipline and let his everyday character rub off on us. Are we letting down this generation and limiting our own spiritual lives by subconsciously skipping a generation in the way we interact with God?

Alas for some young people the reason for lapsing into the comfort and safety of the image of God as a grandparent may well be that their own grandparents represent to them more loving figures than their actual parents.

We've found that times of discussion in the middle of, or before, sessions of worship have been really helpful on these fronts. How do folks 'see' the one with whom they are communicating? Short roleplays may help to explain this concept.

For example:

Replay a standard interaction such as conveying the news that you have just split up with your boyfriend/girlfriend, but each time change the character who is being informed, e.g. close friend, father, mother, sister, shopkeeper, head teacher, youthworker, grandparent, vicar, librarian.

Classically folks notice that many things change dependent on who they are addressing:

- Their posture changes, based on their level of respect for the person they are meeting
- Their language changes, based on the age of the person
- Their sentence structure changes with the formality of the setting
- The depth and detail changes with the level of relationship with the person.

Usually, by the end of this folks are convinced that how you 'see' someone (consciously or subconsciously) has a massive impact on how you interact with them. It also facilitates a useful discussion on how young people 'see' God. Which of those people does God feel most like in their present interaction with him? Which would they like it to be?

Some biblical input is always useful here, perhaps listing many of the truths about who God actually is, or perhaps focusing on one or two in particular that you feel would bring more balance to your group's perception of who God is. Do they perhaps need to see him as 'a consuming fire' as well as their Saviour?

[Come like a child]

> *People were also bringing babies to Jesus to have him touch them. When the disciples saw this, they rebuked them. But Jesus called the children to him and said, "Let the little children come to me, and do not hinder them, for the kingdom of God belongs to such as these. I tell you the truth, anyone who will not receive the kingdom of God like a little child will never enter it."*

> *Luke 18:15–17*

In the midst of our desperation to see young people maturing to both physical and spiritual adulthood do we sometimes treat them too much as adults and deny them the innocence of receiving 'as a child'? In an age where innocence is desperately uncool, do we need to reclaim something of that spontaneous 'couldn't care less' attitude of a young child. It is often us leaders who stifle childlikeness in an attempt to stamp out childishness. As a sort of check-list, here are some of the distinctives of child-like worship from the perspective of the child with thanks to my godson, James, for inspiration.

Honesty – When I feel like crying, I will cry. When I feel like clapping my hands, I will clap with excitement. I won't be trying to impress you or fool you. And I will scream at you when I'm not happy!

Focus – I have an unswerving sense of mission to get to a desired resolution, no matter what the cost in bruises or tears. As I scavenge for my favourite toy, the other toys in the pile become of secondary importance. Distractions just aren't distractions because the prize is just too good.

Exuberance – There is an innate joy in purely being me. I love to move my limbs and squeak random noises. There is something great about just having a body and being alive. Do you not feel it?

Inclusion – The innocent desire to openly share my experience. Hence my ability to play with any other random toddler that I meet in the playground, and be best friends within 30 seconds.

Spontaneity – I have the freedom to act, speak, dance or thump in any way I choose right *now*. It will be unpredictable, but beautiful. I won't be checking for permission before it happens.

I reckon those are pretty challenging words to hold up alongside our worship experiences. Maybe we need some more time crawling around on our knees.

[Qs]

◉ How well do we know the family backgrounds of our young people?

◉ In the light of these, what are their perceptions of who God is?

Things I wish I had been told about worship as a teenager

- What most of the words meant.
- Plugging in a guitar is not a sign of divine power.
- Man looks at the outward appearance, but the Lord looks at the heart. (I'm sure I was told this, but I don't think I ever let that truth apply itself to worship.)
- Clapping is not designed for every beat of a bar (beats 2 and 4, by the way!).
- The chords for most songs are pretty much the same, but they look different because they are in different keys.
- Girls aren't just designed to sing harmonies (read carefully!).
- Worship is for God, not for me.
- Just because a song is loud, it doesn't also have to be fast (and vice versa).
- When playing guitar for sung worship, what your right hand does is probably more important than your left hand.
- Clapping or raising your hands is not necessarily a sign of spiritual maturity.
- My favourite songs may not be the same as everyone else's.

Chapter 9

Time

How can we give a generation with little care for history, or the future, a proper temporal context for worship?

'Live for the moment' is the defining philosophy of this generation. Experiences are seized upon with very little regard for the consequences. Mid-term and long-term planning have long since been jettisoned in favour of short-term 'hits'. The concept that 'now' becomes part of the past and we are on a learning journey through time is completely alien. Anything that may take time to achieve is seen as automatically second rate. If we reduce worship to an experience that is solely about now, where the teaching is purely subliminal, we may well be creating just another drug to which young people eventually become desensitised.

Do we sense that in God's eyes and ears our worship is joined with a long line of worshippers stretching back to the dawn of time? We share some of their DNA and we also share their connection to him who 'was and is, and is to come'. Do we realise that the line also stretches forward to eternity? This is our eternal profession and we shall be there among those in white robes.

> *After this I looked and there before me was a great*
> *multitude that no-one could count, from every nation,*
> *tribe, people and language, standing before the throne*
> *and in front of the Lamb. They were wearing white robes*
> *and were holding palm branches in their hands. And they*
> *cried out in a loud voice: "Salvation belongs to our God,*
> *who sits on the throne, and to the Lamb."*
>
> *Rev 7:9–10*

But we don't have to wait to join with those eternal worshippers. God is outside time, hearing our voices with theirs. We also join our voices with all those who for the next hundred years or so will offer worship while laughing at the strange old songs from the nineties and noughties. I can imagine the worshippers of 2104 chortling.

'Can you believe they still had to put the words on a screen back then? In only two dimensions!!!'

'Can you believe that they spent more time practising and learning new songs than serving their communities?'

'We're trying to get rid of our DJ, but all the old people still like some drum and bass at the early communion service.'

'Can you believe they met in the same building every week?'

'Guitars? How many strings did they have again?'

> We live in a culture that is devoid of much hope, especially for the teenage generation.

It has been said that worship is the carrier of the church's values and stories through the ages. To see my responsibility as not only to this generation but also to the generations to come sharpens my mind when I think what sort of worship experiences I craft and what sort of leadership I model. What works best now may leave a nasty hangover in a few years' time. Functionality rides up against wisdom and truth. What sort of legacy are we going to leave for the next generation of worshippers? Will it be tangible, or will we say: 'Actually, you kind of had to be there.'

You could research local church history to bring a sense of story to who your group are and where they have come from. We seldom stop to realise we would not be here if our predecessors had not been here, in the same spot. Academic as this may sound, I have seen some knowledge of these sort of facts give a group an identity. In a rapidly dissociating generation, the knowledge that they are part of a bigger story – both eternally and locally – has a profound effect on young people.

[Timeline]
Something that greatly helps to lock temporal thoughts into a young person's head is a timeline. You could do this using actual people in a long line to represent various characters, or a sheet of lining paper that can just keep going and going. I suggest drawing historic events alongside the biblical worship history to reinforce the reality of the timeline.

After you pass our current spot in time, you need to just keep the line going and going as far as you can – whether it is out the door and up the street, or round and round the hall or room you are in – to underline our worshipping spot in eternity. If you want, you could represent the positives and negatives of history by using the line as a graph, where positives keep the line above the x–axis and negatives drive it below. You could invite the young people to draw on a section representing the highs and lows of their lives, or if this is impractical do it separately.

The fantastic thing is that once you go past your death you can put that line right up to the top of the graph, in fact way off the scale. I shall never forget the first time I did this how much of a revelation it was for some young people that no matter what ups and downs this life brings they are the merest squiggles compared to the high straight line they are going to be enjoying forever.

[Foretaste]

We must be encouraging young people to let the Holy Spirit – the foretaste – be the driving force in their lives. This always makes me think of those ladies in the supermarket who offer you free samples of yoghurt or ice cream. I always manage to make some kind of valid detour to go back for a second taste, just to check. That little sample of pleasure speaks volumes to me about what is happening when the Spirit is filling us in worship. It is a glimpse of what our lives will be like for eternity, when we get to that great checkout in the sky.

I believe this is where worshipping in the Holy Spirit is at its counter-cultural best. We live in a culture that is devoid of much hope, especially for the teenage generation. It is an age of apathy and inertia, where our feelings of helplessness to change the world breed in us the belief that nothing can change in ourselves either. More and more I hear young people presuming that they will never 'rise above my station' or be able to do much 'with the cards I've been dealt'. But when young people experience that guarantee, that seal of what heaven will be, they can start to see what is yet unseen. The Holy Spirit has been described as the 'present, dynamic power of the age to come' and I pray he will more and more enable young people to say, 'I am determined by the future God has promised, rather than the past I have made.' (Both quotes: Doctrine Commission, *We believe in the Holy Spirit*, p173)

Worship is a beautiful conflagration of past, present and future. Paul gives us a sense of this in Ephesians 1:13-14:

> *Having believed, you were marked in him with a seal, the*
> *promised Holy Spirit, who is a deposit guaranteeing our*
> *inheritance until the redemption of those who are God's*
> *possession—to the praise of his glory.*

And it comes burning through in that glorious old song 'Amazing Grace'.

> *When we've been there ten thousand years*
> *Bright shining as the sun,*
> *We've no less days to sing his praise*
> *Than when we'd first begun.*

In the next section of the book we shall look at some of the distinctives that we should be attempting to weave into worship for young people.

WHERE
we could

Distinctives of

be where

we could be

we could be

Distinctives of
where

Hide and Seek

At church, we were working through the book *Dangerous Wonder* by Mike Yaconelli. We had got to the chapter on daring playfulness, and it was my turn to lead a section. Mike had just tragically died, so I wanted to do something special that did justice to his thoughts in the book. There is a wonderful section in that chapter on how at times God is in effect playing hide and seek with us, desiring that we come looking for him with all of our hearts. I decided doing justice to the theme of daring playfulness required an experiential approach and I needed to be slightly daring.

As with many experiential activities, the challenge is to make it a real experience (rather than an artificial experience). There is a difference between role-playing a situation and actually experiencing it. Someone can experience what it is like to be unable to see by using a blindfold, but that is not the same as experiencing what it is like to be blind. So before we played hide and seek with God, I wanted to discover their attitudes to hiding and seeking. It seemed the only way to do this was to put them in a situation where they had to do some seeking.

As my section of the meeting approached, while everyone was praying I slipped out of the building via a side door. I didn't leave instructions with anyone. There was no safety net. I was determined that this should be an experience for me too.

By the time they said amen, I was gone. At first people thought I was in the loo, but after a quick search they realised something unusual was happening. Several minutes of complete perplexity ensued until someone finally cottoned on to the fact that they were playing a game, and I had left my laptop on my seat. The screen read, 'Hello there folks! I'm hiding. You're seeking! Get into 3 teams. First you need to get the password for wheresflanny@hotmail.com. First to find me gets free cinema tickets.'

Subsequent slides of the PowerPoint presentation were photographs of places in the town centre that had clues hidden nearby. There was a surreal intensity waiting in that coffee shop – not knowing whether anyone was actually playing my game and unable to find out. I wanted the guys to experience the struggles of seeking, and I wanted to experience being sought. Embarrassingly, I was in the loo when the winning team arrived 20 minutes later.

> It was larger than anything I could remember from any previous worship time or preach. In places I would not normally bother looking, I was genuinely seeking God.

Reactions to the experience varied widely so the next phase was particularly potent. Some people had got excited about the game. Some had sat around doing not very much at all, waiting for something to happen. Some had loved the sense of mystery, while some had felt really awkward because there had been a blank space in a meeting. I asked everyone to close their eyes and be silent while I slowly read the following questions:

- Do you revel in the excitement of the unknown, or do you fear it?
- Do you fear not being in control of a situation?
- Seeking, by definition, takes effort. Do we make an effort when we seek?
- Did it feel like an effort to seek after me?
- Does God hide?
- If not, why would he call us to seek him?
- How did your attitude to seeking change when things weren't going so well?
- In general, how much do you let circumstances distract your seeking of God?
- Did it make a difference to your attitude that there was competition and a prize?

Afterwards some folks shared the major things that God had revealed to them and reported that these questions would not have had anything near the same effect on them without what they had just experienced.

Next I played some music and flicked through a series of slides that were biblical references to hiding and seeking. They included

Psalm 10:1
Why do you hide yourself in times of trouble?

Psalm 53:2
God looks down from heaven
on the sons of men
to see if there are any who understand,
any who seek God.

Proverbs 8:17
I love those who love me,
and those who seek me find me.

Jeremiah 29:13
You will seek me and find me when you seek me with all
your heart.

During this folks prayed, read and worshipped.

I explained at the end that the great thing about playing hide and seek with God is that he is inevitably quite bad at it. He desperately wants us to find him. He is always bigger than what he hides behind, and he always has a reason for taking us on the journey.

A completely unexpected result was that in the days and weeks that followed the experience had a profound effect on me. It was larger than anything I could remember from any previous worship time or preach. In places I would not normally bother looking, I was genuinely seeking God. I was looking for him in the unexpected places, and often finding him. There was a joy and a skip in my step because of knowing that God was present in my reality and I could come to him like a child who wasn't too old to play. I kept receiving phone calls from folks at church to register similar experiences in the days that followed.

I learned a lot about going out on a limb, taking risks and letting go of the controls. I think the reality of having a minor crisis that became a shared experience indelibly wrote some powerful truths in our hearts as a group of people.

Chapter 10

Experience

I shouldn't have been surprised by the power of experience. Way back in 1970, Alvin Toffler announced the arrival of the 'experience economy' in his landmark book *Future Shock*.

Being young in 2004 means having experience as your currency. Truth and experience are not seen as competitors, as our parents' generation would have seen them. Interactive and experiential ideas are not just pragmatic, they are intellectually sound. Visual, auditory and kinaesthetic (body and movement associated) learning styles are accepted as distinct and legitimate. Many children have a dominant learning style and until this is discovered and utilised, they will often struggle to keep up with their peers.

We all remember events more vividly and attach emotional significance to them if we participate in them. This is especially true with activities outside our normal pattern. Leonard Sweet says in the book *Postmodern Pilgrims*: 'The frontiers of worship lie in helping postmoderns move, breathe deeply, express emotion, and touch the divine. Postmodern leaders create in the church and especially in worship an "experience economy". I learned in seminary how to craft sermons. I am not learning how to craft experiences.'

So keeping in mind that our purpose is to worship God, not have an experience, let's dive into the experiential world.

A good interactive experience has to 'touch base' with heaven and earth. It must affirm through symbolism that the horizontal and vertical planes of our life are inseparably bonded. A great example is hand-washing as part of worship, usually most appropriate as you start. You can explain how hand-washing can be a physical symbol of something spiritual, essentially that we can confess our sins to God and he washes them away as the dirt is washed off our hands.

Images often have further depths that we can step into, such as the fact that we can't see most of the dirt that is on our hands but we know we need to wash them. There are historical parallels with the bronze basin (Exod. 30:18) of the Tabernacle (see the Ideas section, Page 188). Resonance is also achieved because in the week following the hand-washing we will hopefully wash our hands many times, and the analogy planted by the first washing has a chance of creeping back into the consciousness to enable 'spiritual hand-washing' to be a daily event.

Interactive experiences in worship gain power from our conscious choices in what we touch, taste, shape or draw. There is an intentionality about being physically involved, and worship by its very nature is the choice to choose God in any life situation. The truth is that as humans we all worship 24 hours a day, 7 days a week, 365 days a year. We are made to worship. Worship is our operating system, the first thing installed on our hard drive. We have an innate need to worship. The question is not 'will we worship?' but 'who or what do we worship?'

[New Testament Experiences]
It is worth taking a look at some of the first worship 'experiences' of Jesus' disciples to see if they were head moments – solely the regurgitation of truth – or if they were experiences that engaged all the senses. For the record, and I suspect you will agree with me, Jesus was the best small group leader of all time.

Imagine the Last Supper. Feel it, smell it – the heady mix of awe, tension, reverence, fear, food and wine. Jesus made a point of using the basic building blocks of fellowship – bread and wine – as the earthly permanent reminder of heavenly intervention. There is no better example of the use of stuff of earth to underline the truth. The breaking of bread was so symbolically powerful I doubt any of the disciples were ever able to break bread again without thinking of that moment, reinforced by the sight of his broken body on a cross a few days later. Why has this momentous meal endured for so long as a testament to Jesus' sacrifice? Firstly, Jesus did not speak a set of words to the disciples. He created an experience that impinged on all the senses – touch, smell, taste, sight and hearing. It was key that this was an everyday meal, with everyday ingredients, that could be repeated regularly. Surely this informs our thinking about the visual imagery Jesus would use if he were present in bodily form today? He would not be looking for a complex sanctified icon, but for the profound analogies hidden behind our everyday lives and the objects therein.

A moment when Jesus was at the centre of a worship experience is mentioned in Luke 7. He had been invited to dinner by a Pharisee, who is appalled by what takes place in his house. A woman is obviously crying (wholly inappropriate to start with), but even worse she is wiping Jesus' feet with her tears. And making it really bad, she is known to be living 'a sinful life'. Whose act of worship does Jesus validate? The Pharisee who plays politics, follows the rules and engages in the restating of doctrine; or the physical, experiential, world-oblivious, sinful woman?

So why do we try to worship like Pharisees when Jesus craves us to worship like the sinful woman? What do we model to our young people? Do we hold it together because we have a leadership position, or are we happy to let our thankfulness and worship overflow? Can we embrace the physicality of an act of worship such as this?

Central to the power of experience is the memory of a special moment, a line crossed, a new reality discovered. Stop right now and answer this question. When you think back over your life, which moments stand out? Is it not the case that they all involve some sort of action or physicality that sets the experience apart from the blizzard of information download moments that bombard us?

Fast forward to Luke 8 and you find Jesus and his small group sharing a pretty intense experience – actually, make that a life-threatening situation. Their fishing boat is about to do a Titanic, but the Messiah calls in the special effects. The time and place provide the context for vital words of worship:

> *"Who is this? He commands even the winds and the*
> *water, and they obey him."*
>
> *Luke 8:25*

Perhaps the reason our words of worship often lack immediacy and reality is partly that they are spoken in the safety of a church hall or youth centre. I know that the most powerful times of prayer and worship I had as a teenager were when it seemed as if the future of the world depended on it. When the enemy was quite literally pressing in hard, to sing 'the battle belongs to the Lord' meant a lot more than it had as an abstract way of describing what was going on in the heavenlies. Are we ready to take worship back to the streets? Are we ready to be with Jesus in dangerous situations as well as pleasant ones?

To underline the point, Jesus lays on the ultimate multi-sensory experience for his group in Luke 9. He throws in the works – booming voices, bright lights and the stars of earlier episodes. The event commonly known as the transfiguration shows how God desired a select few disciples to experience his truth as well as hear it. The killer punch lands at the end of this awesome spectacle when a voice from the cloud says, 'This is my Son, whom I have chosen; listen to him.' I suspect I would have listened.

It may be asking a bit much to get both Elijah and Moses to appear at your youth group on the same night (they tend to schedule separately), but I believe we need to take some instruction from Jesus in crafting worship experiences for our troops and encouraging them to do the same for each other.

Sometimes we just need to let our imaginations run a little bit wild so that we can learn to be facilitators of experiences. Here are a few examples.

[Kiwi Crisis]
At a youth camp in New Zealand, participants were being taken between venues by coach. As they drove through the forest, a group of armed men appeared from the trees and flagged the coach down. The men boarded the coach and ordered all the boys to sit on the right and the girls on the left. The boys were then marched off the bus into the forest, while the driver was ordered to continue the journey with only the girls. What none of the young people knew was that the armed men were from the New Zealand Army and were only posing as kidnappers. There was nothing contrived about the fear they felt. It was very real. After a time, everyone was reunited in the main hall and the ruse explained.

The exercise was intended to help them identify with the persecution and separation of Christians in China. The leaders wanted the young people to appreciate their freedom to worship, and suspected that only through experiencing the horror of the situation would it become real to them. Obviously I can't go along with the extremity of this method, but you can see how a genuine experience turns knowledge into understanding. I suspect many of those young people now pray more for the persecuted church than I do.

[Dress Code]

Another, milder, example is from a church in the United States that organised 'the youth event to end all youth events' with a big slap-up, sit-down meal, great videos, games, and the best bands the country had to offer. The venue was a luxurious hotel ballroom. Invitations went out many months before the event, detailing the time, date and location, and very prominently stressing that only those adhering to the dress code would get in. A plan had been hatched.

Young people being young people, during the time between the invites being sent out and the day of the event they forgot about the dress code. Instead they just got more and more excited that they would be seeing their favourite bands like DC Talk for the first time. On the night around 500 young people turned up and were ushered into a dull anteroom off the luxury ballroom.

They could hear the bands doing sound checks and see the expensive lights flickering through the cracks in the screen door. Anticipation was reaching fever pitch. At this point the leader got on to a table and welcomed everyone. Cue loud cheers and more excitement. Then he dropped the bomb: 'As you will remember from the very obvious note on your invites, only those adhering to the dress code will be allowed in. The rest of you will get some crisps and snacks out here.'

A rumble of astonishment turned into complete silence. They couldn't be serious, could they? The forty or fifty people who had dressed properly were led into the youth event to end all youth events while everyone else stood by wide-eyed with their chins on the floor.

'Sorry, but we did make it clear that the dress code was non-negotiable. It's out of our hands. See you next week.' There was a frenzied chorus of 'that's not fair' and 'come on', but the leader disappeared before he could be apprehended. A crowd of very disgruntled young people spent the next twenty minutes plotting, scheming and moaning about their predicament, not-so-quietly seething at the injustice. They knew that just next door the event had kicked off without them. Just as frustration levels in the anteroom were reaching breaking point, the leader appeared on stage again to say, 'Oh, okay then, you can all come through!' The exhilaration of the moment instantly rendered all previous frustration null and void, and the crowd piled through.

Later on someone completed the plan, using it to illustrate what grace truly is and how it is different from qualifying by following the written code. Those who don't deserve to be 'let in' are 'let in'. I suspect the intensity of the experience means that a lot of those young people will never forget the illustration that led them into worship. The gratefulness and genuine relief they knew that night fed into their gratefulness that a God who by all rights shouldn't have, has welcomed them in.

[Sacred Santa]

Here is another experiential exercise that centres on grace. Show everyone a hat and explain it contains the names of all the group members. Ask everyone to secretly select a name from the hat. Tell them that the next week they must bring a present worth no more than £1 for that person. The twist is that all the bits of paper in the hat have the same name on them. That person will even have to buy themselves a present. Seven days later, there will be looks of complete shock and astonishment when the presentation gets to gift number three (number two may have been a mistake) and everyone realises what is going on. This is a perfect opportunity to talk about our attitudes to giving and receiving in the context of worship. People will know exactly what emotions and feelings have just gone through their gut, and the following questions allow some expression of this.

[Qs]

- Do we give only because we expect to also receive?
- How did it feel to not receive something you thought you deserved?
- How do we react to God's free gift to us?

And to the recipient –

- How did it feel to be given what you did not deserve?
- How did it feel to be blessed beyond what you expected?

Challenge: What biblical truth could I reinforce by creating a worship experience?

Hint: To get you going, some subjects lend themselves very well to this such as being lost, being bought at a price, God's protection, etc.

Chapter 11

Community

Nothing could be more radical for young people today than the beautiful instructions given by Jesus in Matthew 5:23–24. 'Therefore, if you are offering your gift at the altar and there remember that your brother has something against you, leave your gift there in front of the altar. First go and be reconciled to your brother; then come and offer your gift.'

There is phenomenal counter-cultural potential for worship in building community, as mentioned in Chapter 1. Our vertical interaction is inextricably linked to our horizontal interaction. Paul underlines this in 1 Corinthians 14:26. 'When you come together, everyone has a hymn, or a word of instruction.'

> If I am singing 'we' then there is more chance of me realising that not only am I coming to God with my brothers and sisters in this room, but with the church at large.

Paul sums up for me one of the distinctives of Christian community. It is not a support group to help us with our self-esteem, but a place where in giving we receive. Unless we consciously channel the power of worship towards community, we build up the 'blessing-shop' model. By this I mean that the experience of worship can become like retail therapy of a spiritual kind. It turns us into fussy consumers who select the worship style and size we like best and then leave. We try to fool ourselves that worship is just about me and him, because it honestly is easier that way. Other people can be so unreliable, and they complicate matters!

Jesus is unbelievable. In the passage above from Matthew he is suggesting that if someone has a problem with me it is my job to take the initiative to start dialogue and reconciliation. Everything within us screams 'I'm not saying another word to him until he apologises', but here Jesus calls on us to swallow our pride and sacrifice our rights for the good of community.

And of course we immediately crash headlong into the reality that many young people have experienced for most of their lives. Most playground and family arguments centre around standing up for 'my rights' or explaining why 'that isn't fair'. Many people's experience of family means that instead of sacrificing for the good of community they choose to avoid compromise. For example, rather than discussing which television station to watch we give everyone their own TV and retreat to our bedrooms. Unfortunately many young people also experience one of their parents making a decision like that to step back from the heat of community permanently.

I believe that true worshipping communities can begin to teach our world what community really is. In post-Thatcher society, young people are only able to make the decisions necessary to create community with the power of a vertical connection and the support of meaningful horizontal connections. It is now nearly impossible to make radical decisions on your own, because a choice doesn't feel like a choice. It's just what everyone does.

This is why it is so important that we do not simply buy into the spirit of the age with our worship experiences. The problem is that this often happens without us realising it.

We have to intentionally create horizontal interaction during our gathered worship times because this helps to take the emphasis off us being blessed. Whenever possible, I believe, we should be earthing in relationships what is going on in worship. If God is dealing with something in me, over the next few days or weeks I am not meant to be able to cope on my own so involving some peers from the start of that process is essential. I cannot forget the impact that being part of a small community had on my early experiences of 'mass worship'. It may be why I cannot settle for impersonal mass experiences these days.

In the words of Battlestar Galactica, we were a 'rag-tag fleet'. A group of about 30 young people from a church in Portadown, we arrived at the Summer Madness festival in 1990 trying to find our way in the world.

We were only loosely affiliated, although we'd been hanging around together for some time as a youth group. There was no sense of deep friendship or intimacy. Over the course of five days I had my eyes opened to the symbiosis between worship and community.

We established our own area where we all sat together during the worship sessions. Woe betide any stray youth wandering into our territory. Any Dayglo Bermuda shorts in that area had to be on Portadown legs.

There was a strong sense of us being on a journey together. We were stepping out into new territory in worship and learning so much about the power of God to change lives in front of our eyes. Every night at the end of the sessions as people waited behind for ministry, we assembled into a large circle and continued to sing or to pray for each other. There was an intensity about those times of prayer that I'm not sure I have experienced since. Everything seemed so vital, and each life that God touched or changed seemed of the utmost value. Many, many tears were shed. One person's joy or pain was felt by the whole group. Stories and secrets long held in the dark came out into the light in a way that meant everyone was resolving to stand with the individual as they fought through whatever it was they were going through.

> People need to experience that it is better worshipping with the whole body than being by themselves in their own room at home.

I have no other way of explaining what happened except to say that in drawing us closer to himself, God very beautifully drew us closer to each other. It was the first time another person's well-being seemed more important than my own. My heart truly broke for each of them as God downloaded his heart to us. The immense blessings we experienced had significance because we were able to share them.

[I Versus We]

Can you see why hunting for more songs that use 'we' instead of 'I' is so important? Inevitably, if an experience is about me connecting with God – *I will give you all my worship, I will give you all my praise* – then any interaction between myself and those around me is incidental or accidental. If I am singing 'we' then there is more chance of me realising that not only am I coming to God with my brothers and sisters in this room, but with the church at large.

Being stuck in an 'I' world when you are physically on your own also belies a theological truth. As Graham Cray says, 'We may worship personally, but we never worship as individuals.' Any time we come to God in worship, we are coming with millions doing exactly the same thing.

I'll say it again, a young person's theology is (whether consciously or subconsciously) built around what they sing. What is their inevitable assumption if they sing many songs asking God to bless 'me' or 'us', and very few asking God to bless others; never mind the poor or the marginalized or the oppressed? As leaders and youth workers we have a responsibility to be to some extent gatekeepers to their lexicon of worship language, assuring balance and at times substituting short-term high for long-term maturity.

[Rolling it Out]

At some stage you may have to explain the rules of being community – there is space for everyone to do their own thing, but at some point you must sacrifice what you want to do for the good of everyone and the group experience. Give examples. A Mexican wave works because everyone joins in. What if no one stood up?

Sowing these thoughts of community is often helped by explaining that we are the body of Christ.

Just as each of us has one body with many members, and these members do not all have the same function, so in Christ we who are many form one body, and each member belongs to all the others.

Romans 12:4–5

It is a truly mind-expanding notion for young people that when they are gathered together they are more than the sum of their collected parts. We need to affirm this reality in our worship. People need to experience that it is better worshipping with the whole body than being by themselves in their own room at home. Here are some ideas you can use to promote this sense of community in worship.

Rhythm

The different voices in a rhythm all play something distinct from the other parts. They have different sounds and are played at different times. But a rhythm only sounds like a full rhythm when all the parts come together. Get folks to play a rhythm together. Use chair-tapping, clapping and hand rubbing, or hand out different percussive instruments. (See the Rhythm section, Page 24 in Chapter 2.)

Interaction
Give folks time to mix. You could try modern versions of The Peace – high 5s and sidearm hugs galore! Sometimes it is useful to keep The Peace inside the context of a song, so that no one picks up a non-verbal message that the horizontal communication is separate from the vertical communication. Small groups could be formed to write words together, or in ministry all those in the vicinity could be asked to lay or point a hand.

Testimony
Create opportunities for people to share what has been happening in their lives with the whole body. Make sure they are prayed for after sharing and updates are given on the progress of different situations so everyone knows there is active purpose in their sharing and praying, as opposed to it being someone's moment in the limelight.

Singing in rounds and harmonies
This is a great example of some things being better with more people involved, even if it does take a bit of effort.

Giving
From a body-consciousness point of view, this is a key act of worship for young people. Try to create a context in which it is all right to share needs, whether within or outside the group. It is important to report back on situations of need they have helped to show the power of doing something as a body rather than as an individuals.

> *"Give to the one who asks you, and do not turn away from the one who wants to borrow from you."*
>
> *Matthew 5:42*

> *Away with the noise of your songs!*
> *I will not listen to the music of your harps.*
> *But let justice roll on like a river,*
> *righteousness like a never-failing stream!*
>
> *Amos 5:23–24*

Doing things in unison
Try reading sections of printed words together. These may be sections of the Bible or song words or liturgical prayers.

Creative responses
Try building a wall from bricks on which each person has painted their name. See the Ideas section for many more.

Strategic gathering points
Ask people to stand together at significant points, such as in front of the cross or before the altar.

Physical body representations
Draw out a body on the ground in a 'crime-scene' way. Folks could place fingerprints or sign their names in the area of the body that they feel they most connect with.

Holding hands
For prayer and for songs. You know best whether this is appropriate for your group. Remember to make it clear when hand-holding is stopping too.

Improvisation
Allow the unexpected to happen and, more than that, allow it to inform the rest of a session. Often folks will need encouragement to go off the script, and explanation afterwards if something new has happened.

Wake-up call

Setting: Early in the morning in a big tent at a festival. It works really well with small groups too, and not just early in the morning.

You know when you have just the edge of an idea in your head, but you can't quite make out what the whole thing looks like? That was what that morning felt like. I knew I wanted to create space for the youth group to actually minister to each other as a community, but I also knew that at 8am they may need a bit of a stimulus to do so.

It suddenly struck me that what really gets me typing or writing is being asked a specific question. Before that I can sit and stare at a piece of blank paper for quite a while. Suddenly it was in my face.

> *When Jesus came to the region of Caesarea Philippi, he asked his disciples, "Who do people say the Son of Man is?"*
>
> *They replied, "Some say John the Baptist; others say Elijah; and still others, Jeremiah or one of the prophets."*
>
> *"But what about you?" he asked. "Who do you say I am?"*
> *Matthew 16:13–15*

He isn't asking who does your church believe I am, or who does your youth group say I am, or who do your parents say I am, but who do *you* say I am? It is the ultimate in-your-face question that demands an honest response, even if that response is 'I honestly don't know who you are' or something even more negative.

After some sung worship, I read that passage and invited folks to answer the question honestly by scribbling on the lining paper that was stretched all over the floor. What happened next bettered my hopes for the session by some way. As suggestions of possible answers to that question cycled through on the screen, and as a DJ followed the mood with some ambient tracks, people grabbed for pens and got down to writing. As people finished their bit they began to wander around the lines of paper, taking in the scene and the words scrawled there. You just knew that the space was being used and cherished.

In the midst of all the action one guy came up to me, visibly emotional, and asked if he could read out one of the bits that he had read. He was blown away because what had been written spoke to him so specifically. To do this he had to rip off a piece of the paper. As he read these words out, I got a strong sense that other people needed to do this too and so suggested folks wander around the words and rip off the piece they felt was designed to encourage or challenge them. The variety of the many different answers to that one question had become an amazing route of communication and ministry amongst a body of people. It was a joyous sound as everyone ripped and kept 'their bit' from the floor.

It was fantastic to finish by singing together 'Holy, Holy, Holy is the Lord God Almighty', further answering that question – 'Who do you say I am?'

[Related ideas]
Show the phenomenal flash presentation based on this question on the CD-ROM from www.highwayvideo.com. Use the question during sung worship. Encourage folks to sing or shout their answers. If some encouragement is needed, shout out 'you are' to help responses flow.

During an event, create a PowerPoint presentation that comprises the phrases that everyone submits to a happy typist. These are then gradually displayed. The same can occur with an overhead transparency.

CHAPTER 12

Creativity

Worship can become like a stagnant pool. Nothing new is flowing in. Nothing new is flowing out. If folks aren't encouraged to give as well as receive in worship, then this stagnancy is compounded. It is so easy to settle into a pattern and rely on a leader to do our thinking for us. How do we get the 'in' and 'out' channels open?

I believe two of the major keys to creativity are looking and listening. Young people are trained by the multiplicity of entertainment options available to them to be sponges. I am writing this in a house that has nearly one thousand TV and radio channels. Most of my day could be spent just cycling through the channels. Young people are continually being entertained, but rarely fulfilled or satisfied. The default activity on coming home from school is flopping on the couch, grabbing the remote, and 'veg-ing'.

> Do we encourage young people to expect creative thoughts to pop into their heads? How do you get that initial spark of inspiration while sitting in your bedroom, and how do you develop it once you do?

Of course we all need relaxation time, but it seems to have become the electronic equivalent of magnolia painted walls – it's just loud enough to let you know that it's there, but has a brain-numbing effect. We are stimulated at a superficial level; enough to prevent boredom, but not enough to inspire creative thoughts. This default mode of being content to suck in all that the world's media spits out increases the mental effort required to write, draw or produce anything creative. When Robbie said 'let me entertain you', we sat down and said 'okay then.' Some of us have yet to get up.

Only when this stream is dammed, or we cease our constant motion, do we truly have time to look and listen. A good challenge for young people is to find a spot where they won't be disturbed for just 15 minutes, and to practise the art of stopping. I certainly need to do this. Once you have stopped, it is hard to believe the detail and beauty you normally miss. They may want to stop on a bench in the high street, or looking out over a valley, or in a crowded playground. There is so much to see in this world, and so much to hear from God about what you see. This is especially useful if you are trying to encourage young people to create resonant worship experiences.

Take the example of a youth group that has been out for a walk on a beach. On returning to church, before some sung worship, one of the young people shares what had grabbed her attention on the beach. She had marvelled that the waves never stop coming. Even with all of our advanced technology, nothing we could build, no matter how wide or powerful, could hold back those waves. She had sensed that this was a powerful image for God's unending love. Phrases from songs like 'your waves of mercy crash over me' suddenly became more meaningful. The fact that the whole youth group had just shared her experience and could understand what she meant enabled them to nod their heads in agreement and identification. The image had a life in their heads and hearts, both for these moments and probably for some time afterwards.

> [It doesn't have to feel spiritual to be spiritual.]

By sitting still in a shopping centre for 15 minutes, another group noticed how many text messages arrived in a small area in a short amount of time. The bleeping was almost continual. This caused a realisation that as young people they were more desperate than ever to feel connected, that they mattered to somebody. Someone shared how often their mood was dependent on how many voicemails, messages or texts they received in a day. Someone else admitted that often their motivation for sending a text message was purely the desire to receive one in return. They posed the question as to how healthy this was, and wondered whether we needed a deeper connection to show us real love. They encouraged their fellow young people to look upon the worship that followed as a connection with God, with mobile and text message visuals to reinforce this. Some folks actually constructed text messages to God. The next week many spoke of how this experience had resonated with them during the rest of their week, when texting. This is the beauty of creative ideas by young people, for young people. There is much less translation required.

The next example involved three young people. They set three chairs in the centre of the room with their backs to each other in a triangle, and then faced outward looking at each of us around the room. There was complete silence and some confusion, but they held their nerve and continued to look (in a non-intimidating way) at various members of the group. After about three minutes of silence, one of them said: 'Have you ever thought about just how closely God looks at you, how he knows every hair on your head, every dimple, every angle? He pays you so much loving attention.'

There was more silence, as everyone appreciated the enormity of what was being said. The exercise had a massive impact because we had just experienced something that reinforced the truth we were being told, and boy did it lead people to worship. The root of their idea had come because they stopped in the high street for long enough to notice how other people sitting were simply staring, taking in every detail of various people or things.

[Backtracking]
It feels to me as if we have invested the greater proportion of our time in the last few years in the final stage of the creative process. Training a band to play songs, for example, or doing dance workshops. Where we have invested least is the start of the creative process. Do we encourage young people to expect creative thoughts to pop into their heads? How do you get that initial spark of inspiration while sitting in your bedroom, and how do you develop it once you do? Young people need to be empowered to believe that they all have creative potential and that creativity is not the sole preserve of leaders, musicians, artists and untouchable famous people. Sometimes all that a young person needs is the encouragement of someone saying, 'That sounds good. Let's try it!' In this context, it is much easier to train and make suggestions on how to make best use of ideas; developing them for the benefit of everyone else.

Another important thing I have been learning recently, and which I am desperate to pass on to young people, is this – it doesn't have to feel spiritual to be spiritual. If a thought or song or activity has worked really well, I try to backtrack to its starting point. I try to locate the exact moment when I thought, 'I wonder if we could…?'

What I am surprised to find is that the first moments of those ideas are fairly innocuous. When I look at what I was doing or thinking at that moment, it usually surprises me by its lack of specialness. There usually aren't any fuzzy feelings, tongues of fire or leaping out of the bath shouting eureka!

I want to encourage young people that there are no mystical powers involved in the creative process, that there are no secrets they don't have access to. It's great for them to know that God planted his creativity in them, and it's all right to let it grow by running with a thought that may not seem to be a life-changing idea. It doesn't have to feel spiritual to be spiritual.

[Definition]

The best definition of creativity I've read is: 'The art of bringing something into being that has not existed before.' It was written anonymously on the floor during a time of worship. Another is, 'Hearing what isn't there yet.' Sharing these broad definitions can often encourage folks who don't see themselves as creative. The new thing could be a new method of seating, or a new structure to the programme, or a new name for the group. Let's not reduce this to art and music.

[Learning from the Master]

Jesus is probably the most creative man ever to walk the face of the earth. He was endlessly creative. A man with such divine power could have caused miracles to happen in the most elementary way, but if you analyse how he acted and interacted there is an intentional poetry about his words and actions. And that's not even counting his many years of creativity as a carpenter.

When Jesus came upon a blind man (John 9) the easiest thing would have been to snap his fingers and announce the man's restored vision. But read what actually happens.

> *Having said this, he spat on the ground, made some mud with the saliva, and put it on the man's eyes. "Go," he told him, "wash in the Pool of Siloam" (this word means Sent). So the man went and washed, and came home seeing.*
> *John 9:6–7*

What Jesus does has so many angles to it. I love this man who is God. He confirms both his humanity, by spitting and mud-making, and his divinity, by a miraculous healing. He is prepared to get his hands dirty. He is prepared to create some natural theatre. He is prepared for the drama and tension to unfold, rather than go for the immediate crowd-pleasing result. The other thing that stands out is that he includes the blind man in the process. His actions of faith become a vital part in his healing. Jesus wants this to be an interactive experience, not something that the blind man has done to him.

> I am constantly amazed by the creativity of this generation of young people. They push out the creative boundaries of worship far beyond anywhere my generation has dared to go.

Before he met the blind man, another moment of intense creativity had just occurred in Jesus' life (John 8). I don't know how you or I would have approached the situation, but I suspect that my actions would not have been as creative as what Jesus came up with. There is a woman who is about to be stoned for being caught in the act of adultery and she is flung in front of Jesus, and the crowd who are baying for blood. Now Jesus could easily have found an elevated spot, pulled himself up to his full height and spoken with such power and eloquence that no one would have dared to lift a stone. But he didn't. He did something that even now gets us talking about what he was doing. And perhaps that's a large part of the point. Anyone who saw the blind man healed or the woman saved would automatically have a hook into their visual memory. It wasn't just words being spoken. Poetic action took place. You and I remember the stories more clearly amongst the myriad stories of our lives because of these visual hooks. When Jesus stooped to write in the sand, I imagine everyone just stopped because something new was happening.

The Creator was getting creative.

[Creativity Killers]

It is good to be aware of the things that kill creativity. The prime culprits I have met on my travels include overbearing leadership, lack of encouragement, quitting after the first 'failure', lack of preparation, failure to 'complete' an idea, laziness, a 'safety-first' approach, and incorrect theological dogmatism.

Many of these creativity killers appear when leaders are in task mode. They occur when our focus is getting through a programme as effectively and efficiently as possible. On top of the proximal effect of stifling experimentation, the effect is to instil wrong values in our young people so they begin to operate in the same way. Allowing too little time for preparation is probably the next greatest stumbling block to creativity, both actual preparation time and time between the planning meeting and the execution. The most creative ideas will often come after the planning meeting, as themes and concepts incubate in minds. Further thoughts may complete an embryonic idea from the meeting. The best creative thinking often occurs when you are not specifically focused on a task. The other advantage is that because these ideas spring up as people go about their normal lives, they are more likely to reference everyone's reality.

> [The shackles that have held my generation
> down for so long are coming off.]

[Outside the Box]

Sometimes when it comes to thinking outside the box we are so conditioned by the 'normal' ways of doing things that we need to take a complete step back to be truly creative. Here are some tips for thinking outside the box.

- Pray – your creativity is God-given, so go straight to the Maker for inspiration. Sorting out creative ideas can at times be taken less spiritually seriously than writing a sermon or choosing songs
- Do it with other people – bounce ideas off each other to filter out the rubbish, see new perspectives and mould each other's ideas
- Get away from your normal space – this may aid you in gaining some perspective
- State the impossible – sometimes it helps to state what you know you can't do. Just modifying that slightly may be your answer. This is similar to stating there are 'no rules' for the discussion
- Have confidence – every idea was new when it started

⊙ Keep asking the 'why?' question about the way you normally do things – and then from the answer work out how else that answer could be reached. It is important to step back as far as possible. For example, a conversation may go as follows: Why do we have a leader? To make sure that sometimes we do the same things at the same time. So how else could that happen?

Here is an example of a creative process that I had the privilege of being involved in recently. I hope it shows how a team approach can be fruitful.

Abbi wanted the focus of her talk to be the lies we believe when we are told them by family, friends or enemies. Lies such as 'you'll never be as good as your sister' and 'see, you've failed again, like always'.

We wanted the sung worship to include something interactive, to reinforce the message and act as a response. As the discussion proceeded, Abbi suggested that these lies actually provide something like a runway for the devil to 'land' on and take over our thinking. One of the girls quickly proposed that we lay a couple of rolls of lining paper on the floor and draw markings on them to create a runway down the centre of the room. Another person realised that fairy lights stretched down the sides would add to the strong visual image. It was then suggested that the young people scribble the lies that they had been believing on the runway.

Now we had a problem though, the rest of the analogy involved us 'bombing' the runway to render it incapable of acting as a landing zone for the devil. Bearing in mind that no one in the group had brought along tactical weapons, we pondered for a moment and toyed with some crazy ideas but none that seemed appropriate. One very silly idea that involved dangerously destroying the paper prompted someone else to rationalise a solution, ripping the paper into small pieces and then putting them back together to form statements of truth. These small bits ended up spelling out words such as 'loved' and 'chosen'. It was very powerful, and could not have happened without prayer, teamwork and lateral thinking.

I am constantly amazed by the creativity of this generation of young people. They push out the creative boundaries of worship far beyond anywhere my generation has dared to go. What encourages me most is that their desire to be like Jesus is stronger than their desire to keep people happy by 'doing the right thing'. It seems the shackles that have held my generation down for so long are coming off.

I am convinced that a smile crosses Jesus' face when we interact creatively with him in worship. He created us with an awesome potential to come up with new things. These may be things that even he hadn't previously thought of. That is what new means. That is creativity. Obviously we use the raw materials he has provided, but it is still an unbelievable thought. Let's rise to the challenge of making his eyes open that little bit wider and seeing him smile.

[Qs]

◎ What aspects of our gatherings or small groups could we ask the 'why' question about? Could some young people be involved in this discussion?

◎ Are you empowering your 'creative thinkers' as much as your musicians?

Void

Setting: Church youth group
Time: Sunday morning

Everyone is very tired, and slightly disappointed after a 'mission' that was not very fruitful. As we worship there is a distinct sense of lethargy and almost of taking everything for granted.

The situation has me asking, 'God, how often do I take you for granted?' So I stopped playing guitar and asked everyone to ponder this question in silence: 'What would your life look like without God? What difference would it make if he didn't exist?'

You could cut the atmosphere with a knife and you could almost feel the cogs turning in people's heads. I left things silent for a few minutes. One by one, the most amazing statements were made by almost every member of the group. The stories ranged from being sure that they would be in organised crime, to being sure that they would be sleeping around to find love, to being sure that they would be long gone by now via an overdose. Tears flowed as people realised the intensity and reality of what was being shared. Because of the stark question, what had previously been something to make life a bit better, causing us to sing in a tepid and fuzzy way, had become the most important fact in the universe and it demanded an honest and total response.

There was also a sudden appreciation for the group they were a part of, for the church they often ridiculed, and for the leadership they had taken for granted.

I used to love the children's story *Grimble*. He was a lad whose father was a signalman at a busy railway junction. Their flat was above the railway lines, so Grimble had never known anything but the constant rumble of the trains underneath. I was especially impressed by what happened to Grimble one summer's morning.

There was a train strike. Grimble woke up with a start. 'Whassat?' he exclaimed, freaked out by the new experience of complete silence.

In the same way, I think we sometimes need a jolt out of our complacency about God's ever-present love and care. Visualising what life would be without him is one way of doing that. It may be good to encourage some creativity on this theme. The musicians especially may like to get their teeth into writing some songs, if you give them a first line like, 'If you were not here... '

Chapter 13

Preparation

An inevitable result of living in the now generation is that planning and preparation are deemed to have little value. Time spent now for a future benefit is time not spent on one of the various opportunities for stimulation that now offers. I guess it's similar to how I feel when I look at a bar of Cadbury's Whole Nut. Every nut represents a waste of potential chocolate space!

Jesus planned meticulously. If ever there was someone who should be able to 'wing it', it was Jesus. But he didn't. Take for example the preparation for Jesus' triumphal entry into Jerusalem.

> *"Go to the village ahead of you, and at once you will find a donkey tied there, with her colt by her. Untie them and bring them to me."*
>
> *Matthew 21:2*

The preparation was creative, intentional and specific, and paved the way for a powerful experience of worship.

Some of the young people I have mentored had an 'it'll be all right' attitude to preparation for worship. This is actually not always laziness, but often a positive trust that God is in control. However, what it also reveals is a shirking of leadership or a fear of being prescriptive for their peers.

> I am all for spontaneity, as my team members will frustratedly tell you, but I recognise how important it is that we don't raise up being 'led by the Spirit' during a gathering above being 'led by the Spirit' two weeks previous while preparing.

Another factor is 'choice fatigue', by which I mean that our consumerist culture has bombarded us with so many choices that we are no longer able to choose. To choose is to make a commitment, and many young people find commitment innately negative. They prefer the tension of not knowing to the prison of commitment, even when it's something they want.

I see a lot of this in myself. I want to keep all options open until the last second, but I've noticed that when I sit down and give some prayer and preparation time to a gathering the positive effects are tangible. I am all for spontaneity, as my team members will frustratedly tell you, but I recognise how important it is that we don't raise up being 'led by the Spirit' during a gathering above being 'led by the Spirit' two weeks previous while preparing.

Perhaps part of the problem is that preparation can be a private thing, and we would rather spend time on things that other people can see us doing to prove that we are worth having around. It has been said that 95 per cent of what God does in us he does behind our back. Could we aim for something similar?

> Jesus was continually explaining to the disciples the full extent of what was going to happen when they reached Jerusalem.

Including a core team in times of intentional preparation, even when you already have a strong idea of where an event is headed, can bear much long-term fruit. It's often not possible to teach someone how to help people think creatively, they have to catch it. Group brainstorming enables folks to experiment with ideas and make contributions in a safe environment with balanced leadership, which is often different to the task-driven youthful exuberance of a young leader with a guitar strapped around them. Folks can be discipled and blessed by the process and not just the product. In the context of calm worship planning meetings, we have seen people speak up who would never normally have a voice in a music practice. This dynamic also heads off the tunnel vision of a band arriving solely to play music. It lets everyone stop for a moment to think about what they want to achieve and why, and what the best tools for that will be. If music and songs still form part of that then great; but at least they have been chosen for a reason.

Specific preparation was required for the Last Supper. Note again the empowerment involved. The detail of this meal was to echo for eternity.

> *So he sent two of his disciples, telling them, "Go into the city, and a man carrying a jar of water will meet you. Follow him. Say to the owner of the house he enters, 'The Teacher asks: Where is my guest room, where I may eat the Passover with my disciples?' He will show you a large upper room, furnished and ready. Make preparations for us there."*
>
> *Mark 14:13–15*

Even looking back to the start of his ministry, Jesus put in immense preparation by spending forty long hard days in the wilderness. Add to all this the fact that Jesus was continually explaining to the disciples the full extent of what was going to happen when they reached Jerusalem, and you get the picture of a spontaneous, Spirit-led man with an emphasis on preparation.

The next chapter may be helpful in giving you a framework for preparation.

Chapter 14

Themes

Communication style is one of the key areas where postmodernists and youth workers intersect. We have mostly moved away from three-point sermons, which go from point 1 to point 2 then to point 3 in a linear, academic way. We have arrived at the one-point sermon, which attempts to make a central point via the use of much illustration and story-telling. The changes in audience receptivity and memory are huge. Similarly, it can be very effective for worship sessions to have thought-out themes at their core. It is good to be able to look back and know you met with God, but to also be able to say, 'Yes, it was all about light and darkness'. This core memory will lead to associated memories of the other aspects of the event.

Here is a useful framework for incorporating themes, or in fact for planning for any worship gathering.

[Preparation]
Is there something that everyone could be asked to bring, related to the theme?

Or something they could write, draw, make, or tear from a magazine?

[Environment]
What venue will you use? Do you need to be tied to one venue? Does it need to be indoors?

How can the décor reinforce the theme? Could it become part of a creative response (e.g. everyone takes a stone home with them)?

Will it be best for people to be mostly standing or sitting?

On chairs or cushions?

In small groups or one large group?

Can the interior be used to spring an appropriate surprise at any point (e.g. Ah..., that's why that was hanging there)?

Can you separate the venue into different areas for different activities?

Are there various set-piece objects that interact with the theme that could be placed around the venue?

[Music]
Are there tracks that are particularly applicable or which create an atmosphere conducive to the theme?

Are there any sound effects or spoken word recordings that would be effective?

Are there any corporate worship songs that fit, and would there be a creative way to use them (e.g. singing 'Jesus, be the centre' while formed in a circle)?

[Visuals]
Could appropriate video or still images be cycling to reinforce the theme?

Could appropriate art be displayed around the venue?

[Bible]
What are the passages that are key to the thrust of the session?

How could they be represented appropriate to the theme (e.g. 'Go and sin no more' written in some sand on the floor)?

Are there other related verses that could be displayed more simply?

[Story-telling]
Could a group member or leader share some experience connected to the theme?

[Questions]
What are the obvious questions that will get beneath the theme, and earth it into everyday life for a young person?

Could you provide some moral dilemmas, or roleplays?

[Communal Moments]
Are there moments where there is a sense of community from everyone doing, or saying, or singing the same thing?

[Space]
Is there space and time for reflection, perhaps using silence?

[Activity]
What memorable activity could connect people with the theme (e.g. making slings for each other when the theme is 'pain')?

[Ministry]
Is there an opportunity for prayer and ministry? Again this is more easily facilitated with young people if it is also themed, and not simply a generic 'pray for me' session. Young people are more likely to respond if a specific question has been asked. Also, if young people are ministering to each other the central theme gives them confidence as a starting point for prayer e.g. 'Lord, Steve wants to know more of your fire in him, would you turn the sparks he has in his life into a raging flame, etc.'

[Rollout]
Is there something to take home? A postcard, a piece of art that you have created, or a flower (theme: growth)? What would remind someone of the theme in the next seven days?

Is there a challenge, based on the theme, to be carried out over the course of the next seven days (e.g. taking a photo of an effect of the sun – theme: heat, or giving away a possession – theme: sacrifice)?

Elemental themes (such as earth, wind and fire) are particularly strong as they provide lots of potential physical imagery. Set yourself the task of centring an event on one of these themes.

Workshop

I recently had an amazing afternoon with some fantastic young people. They were to lead the worship at an evening meeting on their home turf and had arrived for a music workshop. Everyone got straight to setting up their instruments, and I got a gut feeling that this wasn't what needed to happen.

To their surprise I said, 'Let's just have a chat first.'

We sat uncomfortably in a circle and they were rather unresponsive.

'So,' I said. 'Why do we do all this anyway?'

Gradually answers began to come as I poked and prodded around subjects such as who worship is for, the imagery and language we use, and how we connect these experiences to our everyday lives. When I asked them how the crowd of attenders normally contributed to the evening, there were blank stares. Thoughts of connection and a vague sense of interaction were sliding over their heads. It was clear that even this environment of discussion was a little alien to them.

> [Nothing excites me more than young people being released into leadership and the depths of what God has for us in worship, rather than just paddling at the edge.]

Eventually people felt comfortable enough to chat about their frustrations with the young people they were entrusted with leading. Suddenly the issues that they were complaining about – apathy and lack of focus from the 'punters' – were revealing the need to take on board those new concepts of interactivity and resonance. A really beautiful thing started to happen. Lights were coming on in their eyes as they listened to each other.

They were given a chunk of time to fill with creative ideas in and around the themes we had discussed. Leaving the room was then the most important thing that I could do, so I did.

I have never been so blessed by a group's enthusiasm to apply what they have just discovered. Creative thinkers who had never usually had a say were suddenly the ones being sent off to 'complete' the task while the group leader, stepping up to the plate in an admirable way, was leading the discussion into uncharted waters for himself. In the space of a very short time, they came up with a great idea that exemplified much of what we had talked about that afternoon. But most importantly, it was their idea. They had taken ownership of it and were wanting to make it work, with a focus that was absent from their standard trotting out of songs written by someone else.

> People often don't realise a certain form of expression is even possible until you have obviously 'allowed' it.

It got to the stage that I really didn't care how the ideas for the event went in the end as so much of worth had been achieved simply in the process of their team discussions and planning. They were already resolving to 'do things this way more often'.

As it happened, it was very powerful. In the midst of a sung worship time, folks were divided up into groups of six or seven. Each member was given a piece of thread to hold, which represented them – their gifts and abilities, their history, everything that they brought to the group – and they were invited to tie all the threads in the group together to form a circle when they felt able. Each person then held this circle tightly and prayed for the other members of the group, in the context of more sung worship. Gradually each group then laid their circle of threads onto an OHP screen on which 'JESUS' was written while everyone sang 'Jesus, be the Centre'. This emotive image of a maze of raggy threads held together by Jesus remained on the wall during the rest of the session and added a tangible depth to the worship. Folks said that there was a greater awareness than usual of why they came together as a body to do this. Brilliant. Nothing excites me more than young people being released into leadership and the depths of what God has for us in worship, rather than just paddling at the edge.

[Forum]

One of the most important realisations that sprang from the time the team spent together in preparation was that each of them had similar reservations and frustrations about what took place each week as worship. But because they had not taken the time to stop and chat, assessing what was going on, they were stuck in a rut of doing it 'the way we always do'. This meant that no one had the chance to exercise their obvious giftings in critiquing and analysing the physical and spiritual dynamics of what was going on.

The other impact of this process was that for the first time the team actually took on some responsibility for the way things were. This was not a context for moaning, as snatched conversations in ones and twos can be, but a place where having once identified the issues they felt obliged and in fact wanted to sort them out.

It is very helpful to give young people ownership of not only the leading but also the planning of worship sessions. Only then is a level of responsibility assumed not only for functionally making things work but also for problem-solving and strategising.

However there is no point in giving folks ownership of a process if you do not release them to run with their own ideas and make mistakes. You may have to release a new team to start with no 'givens', so what is created truly feels as if it is theirs and they will take responsibility for making it work rather than feeling like caretakers. You will have a key role in 'allowing' certain activities or ideas. I don't mean rubber-stamping or okay-ing an idea once it has been checked for theological soundness. People often don't realise a certain form of expression is even possible until you have obviously 'allowed' it. For example, with the group above the ideas only really started flowing after I told stories about writing sins on pieces of paper, throwing them in a bin and burning them. (Some of the lads got worryingly excited at that point!) It allowed them to think outside their normal boundaries.

I am passionate about seeing young people thrown in at the deep end in contexts like this. It is not just because it is a progressive, empowering thing to do, but I actually think it is vital in determining whether or not they are still involved in the church in five or ten years time. Perspectives change when people are able to see that church is not simply about being a worship consumer for the rest of their life. Once you involve someone appropriately in any structure

or organisation, they have a vested interest in keeping the dream
alive and they begin to share a desire to see it flourish.

Chapter 15

Personality Types

Personality typing uses an extensive series of questions to uncover your personality 'preferences'. When the Youth For Christ team was being typed I kept thinking that an appreciation of young people's preferences for information gathering, interacting and decision making could be a great help in crafting balanced worship experiences for them.

Please note that we are discussing preferences, not stereotypes. Preferences don't apply in every situation, but seem to hold true if you look at the overall picture of a person's actions and reactions. Here I apply some of the classic characteristics to worship. You may well see yourself or some of your young people in here.

[Extroversion/Introversion]

As a general rule, extroverts focus their attention externally, while introverts focus their attention internally. The question is often phrased as, 'Where do you get your energy?' (This is not an extrovert in the 'talkative' sense of the word.)

Extroverts find God at work first in the 'outer world', through things like events and times when they can talk through an experience. They find long periods of reflection and quiet difficult, but without withdrawing to these spaces can become shallow. They are likely to take initiative.

Introverts, on the other hand, do their processing internally and will not necessarily find it easy to communicate this to others. They will tend more towards private prayer, and become excluded if not encouraged to contribute. They often communicate best in writing, and focus in depth on what catches their interest.

Do we inadvertently promote the extrovert teenagers of a group, assuming extroversion to be a spiritual gift, to the detriment of those who are more introverted?

[Sensing/Intuition]

This preference axis refers to how we take in information.

Sensing folks tend to get caught up in worship through all five senses; for instance through movement or appreciating creation. They may have favourite scriptural texts that will encourage them to worship. They may not, however, always see the connection between the external and internal. Sensors appreciate God in the stuff of here and now; in the washing up and eating. They tend to appreciate Mark's Gospel as it is not full of imagery.

For folks whose intuitive preference leads, God is seen more as creator and cosmic. Ideally there are fewer words involved and more imagination and symbolism. They are very comfortable trying new things, but also need discipline to stay at anything for long enough to go deeper. John's Gospel appeals most here. They trust their inspiration and imagination and are more oriented to possibilities than facts.

[Judging/Perceiving]

The other axis I will apply to worship is in the realm of outer activity.

'Judgers' like to be organised, scheduled and systematic. They connect best with worship that has been mapped out by a leader, and has a logical start and end point. They are energised by completion.

'Perceivers' are spontaneous, flexible and adaptable. They connect best with sessions that are unplanned and open to move in any direction. They desire to experience and understand, rather than control.

These are valid differences. We need to be careful that we are not always organising things in a way that suits our preferences without taking into consideration those at the other end of the spectrum, as that is where many of our young people may be.

[Qs]

- Do you recognise where you are on the three axes?
- Where do you think most of your young people are?
- Is this reflected in the balance of their worship experiences?

Ref: *Introduction to Type* (sixth edition), Isabel Briggs Myers

Chapter 16

3-D Worship

Who do we address when we worship? Young people are confused and always ask me about this. In prayer and song we use the words Jesus, Father, Lord and Spirit interchangeably. Where does one end and another begin? Is it all right to call God whatever we like, when we feel like it? Would it help to grapple with some theology?

I feel the answer to that last question is a resounding yes, especially since so many songs focus exclusively on Jesus and often on just one or two aspects of his divinity. If these songs are all we sing, then the Jesus we worship becomes dangerously separated from the Father and the Spirit. We create a boyfriend/girlfriend figure. Robin Parry has described it thus: 'We end up shallow with worship that, like a bottle of Coke, makes us feel briefly full and content, but one burp and it's gone.'

> Seeing things in their true context ensures we are worshipping the Christian God; who is Father, Son and Holy Spirit.

One of my favourite thoughts is that God is a team. His very essence is a continually interdependent, inter-relating being. Team seems to be a helpful description for young people to grab on to. Our model for love, service and worship is right here in front of us, if we choose to look at him for long enough.

If you are looking for a soundbite, you could say that we always approach the Father in worship through the Son and in the Spirit. Thanks to Robin Parry again.

For through him we both have access to the Father by one Spirit.

Ephesians 2:18

I love the truth of Jesus being our access to the Father, but also our fellow worshipper. We worship the Father with Jesus. In fact he is the perfect worshipper and the perfect worship leader. If all our worship focuses solely on Jesus, we by definition miss this deep and beautiful truth.

I have always struggled with what it truly means to be spiritual in a Christian sense, and it struck me one day that a simple but interesting definition might be 'someone who is like the Spirit'. In other words someone whose life exists not to bring glory on themselves, but to point people to Jesus. Through all of Scripture, this is what the Spirit exists to do. By his power and prompting we are able to escape our selfish natures to speak words and live lives that are worship to Jesus. Perhaps this thought can influence how we pick through the confusion of whom we address when we worship.

Songs of a more trinitarian character allow us to step into the amazing devotion that Jesus showed his Father, and encounter his driving desire to do only his Father's will. The only begotten Son leads the way for us adopted sons and daughters into that loving circle of passion and joy.

In an age where more and more young people are experimenting with alternative spirituality, this is a fantastic distinctive. Seeing things in their true context ensures we are worshipping the Christian God; who is Father, Son and Holy Spirit.

There is a worship idea called 'Trinity Talking' on Page 191 that we have used to good effect in reinforcing these themes.

Chapter 17

The Eyes Have It

[Video – Play]
We are working with a generation upon whom visual stimuli have a massive impact. Images dominate their recognition and thought patterns. Though much of me tries to fight it, I know I am becoming a child of this generation – more likely to lift a magazine than a book, and not entertained unless something is loud and colourful.

For too long we have ignored the importance of visual stimuli in worship, mostly because we are suffering an anti-iconic hangover. What we rest our eyes on plays a large part in what goes on in our minds, and affects our bodies. Being inspired by a diffuse image on a screen may well be preferable to being inspired by the cuteness of certain musicians. We also know the importance of visualisation in memory, so if video material is used thoughtfully it can leave helpful echoes that would not otherwise be there.

> The increased use and diversity of realistic and artistic images of Christ are helping to broaden our minds beyond the standard white Anglo-Saxon Jesus.

We've got to move on from regarding video material as digital wallpaper. It can underline general themes or provoke response, intentionally pushing an 'inward' concept out into the open. In general the images should be strong enough to lead, but diffuse enough not to control people's thinking.

A good use of video recently was inspired by the track 'Lost' by Good Charlotte. We were staying at a conference centre that had a garden maze with high hedges and shot five minutes of footage from the perspective of someone lost in the maze. It was an attempt to encapsulate that frustrating feeling of turning one way, then the other, yet never finding your destination. When shown during worship, some folks found the clip reconnected them strongly with a sense of gratitude that they were found, and others that it refreshed their sense of what it is for a young person to still be lost and re-ignited a passion to pray for them.

The guys at One Small Barking Dog have long been blazing the trail in providing quality visual resources for worship. Check out the videos available on their website. The clip on www.youthwork. co.uk/resources/ is from Images 4. I also recommend a visit to www. highwayvideo.com to buy their excellent video resources, many of which are specifically designed for worship, on various themes.

[Video – Record]

Encourage members of your group during the course of a week to record images and scenes that could provoke or inspire others to worship. It is easiest to set them a theme, such as power, sacrifice or surrender. Allow them to explain what they have recorded.

[Still Images]

With the plethora of images widely available on the net, or from CD-ROM, there is now no excuse for not using them. People often comment on how a certain image used behind the words of a song was helpful, reinforcing the theme, bringing a new angle to the words, helping them to remember it. Creative thought is sometimes required so the images are not used in a clichéd and obvious way. In my song 'How does it Feel?' (primarily about the enormity of the cross and the incarnation) the words of the final verse are

> *Will you teach me how I can follow this way?*
> *How a love so large could fill me?*
> *I get my life, to give it away.*
> *To live is Christ, but to die is gain.*

The obvious image to throw up behind these words would be a snapshot of the crucifixion, but I wanted to come in at more of an angle. For some reason that enduring image of the sole protester standing in front of a column of tanks in Tiananmen Square sprang to mind. Suddenly the words took on a new earth-bound resonance – 'Will you teach me how I can follow this way? I get my life to give it away.' I think images like this can be very important in bringing home the truth of words we happily sing as if they referred to some fuzzy, suspended unreality.

A great way of getting young people involved is by delegating the creation and collection of such images to those among them who are image-savvy. This may involve net-surfing, or getting keen photographers to shoot thought-provoking and inspiring photographs in your own neighbourhood. A list of image websites is on www.youthwork.co.uk/resources/ along with a selection of excellent free images to whet your appetite. Click on the 'Images' section.

> Part of me wants to stand against the tide of needing an image of God to be able to worship him. He is other than us and he is spirit, which means two or three dimensions cannot hold him.

There are many cheap CD-ROMS in software stores with thousands of generic pictures. A quick wade through these can reveal some gems that will specifically suit topics that you are working with.

[Visualisation]

Bearing in mind the importance of visual imagery, it is worth discussing how young people actually visualise the God they worship. Do they have a specific image of God or Jesus in their heads? Often they do, but these differ widely between people. The biggest proportion of those whom I have asked say they visualise a Jesus that is somewhere in their memory; a stained glass window, a crucifix, or a painting. There is not a fixation with this image, but it is certainly the default mode for many. The increased use and diversity of realistic and artistic images of Christ are helping to broaden our minds beyond the standard white Anglo-Saxon Jesus.

Others don't have an image at all, while some report visualising an ethereal cloud-residing God who most of the time does indeed have a white beard. It amuses me that youth workers spend so much time in schools telling people that God is not like the God of *The Simpsons*, but the truth is that some of us still aim our worship at someone who looks suspiciously like him. As we learned in Chapter 8, how we see God powerfully affects how we interact with him. One young person told me he could never visualise Jesus' earthly face because he associated it with being told off by a parent who scolded, 'Jesus wouldn't like you doing that, would he now?'

Due to our increasing individualism and our desire for the purest 'hit', there is a temptation to dissociate ourselves from the crowd during times of sung worship. The classic way we do this is by closing our eyes, so we share the continued aural stimulation but retreat to our own visual world where our mind can write what it wants on our 'blackboard' – the blackness that appears when we shut our eyes. Sometimes it is on this blackboard that God draws pictures or highlights words, which is fantastic, but if this is my only regular worship experience then 'my' God becomes more and more personalised, and I become more and more convinced that the God I draw on my blackboard is the only true image of God, to the exclusion of everyone else's.

He can be exactly what I need him to be. The consumer's ideal God. Through encouraging young people into more dialogue and communal prayer, displaying images for all to see, and just sometimes leaving our eyes open, we will learn to see the Spirit moving in others and keep our worship experiences rooted in reality. We then give God the space to be who he is, rather than who we imagine him to be.

Too many young people have had an intense experience of something they badly needed but subsequently wandered away because the giver of good gifts ceased being the sugar daddy of their imagination. From my experience, young people have more of a chance if they have worshipped him in spirit and in truth, and by 'in truth' I mean that they are worshipping the true God and not some kind of designer 'have it your way' God. Tom Sine describes this kind of God as simply a 'devotional lubricant for the gear changes of life'.

Part of me wants to stand against the tide of needing an image of God to be able to worship him. He is other than us and he is spirit, which means two or three dimensions cannot hold him. I don't subscribe to the idea that seeing is believing, even if it does help sometimes.

[Electronic Worship]

There has been massive change in the world of electronic media. I am interested not purely because young people are drawn to new technology, but especially because the major step-changes that have occurred have been with regard to interactivity.

In 40 years we have gone from radio (listen only and only to what is being broadcast) through television, which added moving pictures and then colour, to broadband internet's brave new world of two-way any-time on-demand communication.

Computers have completely redrawn the boundaries between suppliers and consumers, opening mass media to the masses. Not only can we suck in all the data we want, but we can step into the medium and be part of what is going on. We can be the audience and star of the show. We really can influence what is happening.

We have unlimited potential for sharing worship ideas, multimedia presentations, and online worship experiences. We can even attend one of the recently launched virtual churches.

There are fantastic online resources for personal/small group worship. The development of Flash scripting has led to an explosion of interactive web content that doesn't just stimulate, but invites participation. Check out the 'Flash' section on www.youthwork. co.uk/resources/ for details and to see some samples.

Flash is a great way to get some of your more computer-savvy folks involved in worship. Set them the task of creating flash-based worship material for an event, or for people to use personally. Tuition on getting going with Flash can be found on the website.

Perhaps set a theme such as 'perfection' or 'broken' to get visual concepts stirring. You may want to allow some folks to start off simply, perhaps with PowerPoint presentations. Again, there are many examples of creative PowerPoint presentations on the website.

Chapter 18

Songs For The Pit

It has never been so important to both write songs for young people and encourage them to write songs.

'Give me the songs of a nation and I care not who writes its laws,' wrote Andrew Fletcher, the English political writer, in 1704. With 24-hour-music television in the driving seat of youth culture, how much more vital are songs today?

Songs communicate in a way that words never can; sneaking past the barriers, strongly informing belief and value systems whether we realise it or not. Songs have longevity, hovering in our heads long after their sell-by date.

> Many young people are literally at the bottom of a pit of dark and hopeless emotions while we safely peer over the rim and sing our songs to cheer them up, remind them of a few home truths and make them realise that life is much better 'up here' where we are.

Sometimes the challenge is declined because there's an unhealthy mystique around songwriting, causing it to be seen as an 'experts only' enterprise. I hope the songwriting workshop on www.youth-work.co.uk/resources/ helps to pull back the wizard's curtain.

It's a useful exercise to ask your songwriters to bring in what they feel have been the significant chart tracks of the last few months, and analyse the issues behind the lyrics.

For example: 'Take me Away' – Avril Lavigne, speaking of alienation. 'In the Shadows' – The Rasmus, speaking of lack of purpose. 'Mad World' – Gary Jules, speaking of depression. Each of these songs has struck a chord with the young people I know.

How many worship songs do we know that address these issues?

A strong sense of identification and trust is generated when a lyric connects with a young person's issues, and my prayer is that this healing dynamic will be built up by Christian songwriters as well as mainstream writers.

The gut-wrenching lyrics of Evanescence's 'Bring me to Life' connect powerfully with this generation. There you have the powerful, dark, blood-curdling experience of someone meeting God with intense honesty. Where are the worship songs with lyrics like this? One place you can definitely find them is in the book of Psalms. Nearly half the psalms are songs of lament or poems of complaint. The Israelites and the early church were not into pretence.

'Hope is rooted precisely in the midst of loss and darkness, where God is surprisingly present,' Walter Brueggemann says. 'The reason the darkness may be faced and lived in is that even in the darkness, there is One to address.'

A key attitudinal shift is required here. Many young people are literally at the bottom of a pit of dark and hopeless emotions while we safely peer over the rim and sing our songs to cheer them up, remind them of a few home truths and make them realise that life is much better 'up here' where we are. We need more songs that lyrically get down into the pit with them and identify with some of the causes of their depression and apathy. I think most of us can connect with that place, and if we can't perhaps we need to spend less time doing 'Christian' work and more getting to know a very broken and very hurting world.

It doesn't matter how unqualified you feel. If there is a set of circumstances in a group or a church that need to be reflected but nothing from outside seems to relate, then whatever you write will be much more powerful than anything you can 'buy in'. There is identification with the theme and context, and any performer will tell you that there's a massive difference between performing cover versions and performing your own songs. The sense of fulfilment and the communication are very special.

So don't sit back and just sing someone else's words because song writers are on a higher spiritual plane. Believe me, we aren't! Get writing.

MECHANICS

mechanics

Mechanics of

Distinctive Worship

mechanics

mechanics

mechanics

Distinctive Worship

mechanics

Chapter 19

Crowd Control?

Around the UK, I have observed some excellent spiritual mentoring of young people involved in leading worship.

Unfortunately, an awareness of the practical dynamics of an environment is rarely passed on from mentor to mentee. This is sad because it is a valuable awareness, often putting the icing on the cake. It enables a gifted young leader to see fruits of her labours and take the next step up in responsibility, dealing with extra-curricular factors.

Can a group hear themselves sing?

What is the point of being together to worship if you can't even hear the sound of your own voice, never mind the voices of those around you? There is power in experiencing those around you doing exactly what you are doing. In a band context, it usually comes down to logistics of instrumentation and sound systems.

A good first bet is often to calmly ask the drummer to play more quietly so that everyone else can turn their amps down, so that the sound engineer can turn everything else down through the PA. Training musicians to play without hearing as much of themselves as they'd like is an awkward but important task.

Can all the group read all the words?

Are they big enough and clear enough? Don't use technology for the sake of it. I have been at so many meetings where so many systems of word projection via computer weren't flexible enough to facilitate freedom for a worship leader to change songs or move within a song. I know this is partly operator dependent, but if an OHP does the job without this fuss then don't knock it. For people with reading or text recognition difficulties, serif fonts such as Times

New Roman with tipped and curved ends are much easier to read than more modern fonts.

This leads us into the critically important area of operating the sound and multimedia systems. It cannot be emphasised enough how wonderful it is if the people in both these roles are natural worshippers and valued as vital members of the group, being included in the preparation times. It is essential that whoever does the words also knows the songs and visuals that are to be used so they can spot song and structure changes.

Is the key too high?

People often recoil from changing the key of a song, presuming that it is too much effort, but swapping between keys is in fact relatively simple. Songs today are written and performed for recording in keys that suit the vocal peformances of professional singers with much wider ranges than Joanna and Joseph Public. This unfortunately leaves the songs with intolerably high melodies that most girls cannot sing.

Most songs can retain their energy even when dropped two or three semitones. When I conduct songwriting workshops, I encourage folks that it is in their best interests to write songs that everyone will be able to sing at full-blooded full volume! I would say the absolute highest note in a song should be the 2nd D above middle C, and preferably not above the C above middle C. A great example of a song that retains its energy at the top of the chorus while remaining universally singable is 'My Jesus, My Saviour'. The note for 'Shout (to the Lord)' is B♭ – perfect.

> Knowing a song so well you can play it with your eyes closed facilitates more worshipful playing and greater focus on God.

The freedom of being able to play a song in many keys is profoundly useful for any developing musician as it greatly increases their awareness of the musical position of a chord in a certain key. As this awareness grows, they can develop to the point where they intuitively feel what chord is coming next in any key, have much less need of music, and therefore have more brainspace for leading others and worshipping, themselves (comma important!).

One reason you may want to change the key of a song is to put it in the same key as the preceding or succeeding song, allowing one song to segue into the next. This can be very effective in maintaining the flow of a sung worship session, preventing folks from 'zoning out' between songs.

Detailed instruction on learning to understand the relative positions of chords is available on www.youthwork.co.uk/resources/.

Encourage all your musicians to set themselves the challenge of developing their gift so that they can play without music. Quite often folks don't actually need their music, but use it as a form of safety net. Removing that intent stare towards the paper enables much better communication between band members. Knowing a song so well you can play it with your eyes closed facilitates more worshipful playing and greater focus on God. I have at times mischievously removed all the music, and folks have actually found it amazingly encouraging to look back and see how much more they had in their heads than they thought. I encourage all sung worship leaders to memorise the words and chords of the songs they lead. The extra freedom this gives is vital in leading a band and a congregation, and leaves precious headspace for God to speak into.

Are we arranged appropriately?

Pews were invented after the Reformation in a worried attempt to increase reliance and dependence on the priest. The inevitable breakdown of community was seen as a profitable side-effect by those wanting to quell the 'voice of the people'. Pews are a very effective crowd control tool and we are still experiencing the consequences. But before we throw too much mud at our predecessors, we should check that we aren't creating new versions of old control patterns.

Analysing the physical environment within the paradigm of contemporary worship is a useful exercise. Club culture, with its random groupings spattered across a dance floor, is actually a much more celebratory medium. The freedom of the space and the feel of the rhythms and tracks actually lend themselves much more to celebration. You also find microcommunity and macrocommunity well represented. Small groups of 2-6 people dance in the same area and a larger group is scattered across the whole floor, joined by the shared experience. In clubs you also find people spending time on their own, then rejoining a group. Folks will be dancing near each other then shift and move to somewhere else in a very fluid model of interrelating.

Contrast this to most worship gatherings. They are based on the performance model of a crowd facing a stage. Even though we loudly proclaim that it is not a performance, anyone entering from outside our subculture immediately assumes that this is what is going on. All the elements are there – rows facing front, sound blaring one way, screens facing one way, lights on the band, leadership from the front. In a club the visibility of the 'leader', the DJ, is not paramount. Like it or not, structure and form inevitably feed thoughts and presumptions into young people's minds about what is going on, and whether they have a role in the process.

> Sometimes just a few people experiencing a release to truly express themselves in worship acts as a release mechanism for everyone else.

As long as there is a physical gap between stage and floor, or front and body, there is a psychological gap. This is inherently unhealthy for those on both sides of the gap. Those trapped on the stage side can easily slide into pride and focus on 'product' rather than God, while those left on the floor side can assume their role is to be sponges, always receiving and expecting to never have to give.

[Practicalities]

Should we use seats or sit on the floor? Seats help young people be slightly more focused but may encourage a classroom mentality, especially if they are in regimented rows and columns. Seats may make it easier to get everyone together at the beginning, but make it more difficult for folks to 'find their own space' or respond without embarrassment. Seats obviously don't help if you want to dance. Being comfortable on the floor may make folks more open to receive from God, but also more likely to fall asleep.

I have been part of very powerful worship experiences where folks have been seated in the round, i.e. in concentric circles around a central point or area. There are various things you could place in the middle; such as a cross, an empty chair, or a table set out akin to the Last Supper. These are often helpful as focal points or icons. Songs that most people know are the most useful in these contexts, as it is obviously hard to place a screen for all to see. Just as importantly, well-known songs free people up to acknowledge each other as community together rather than staring at words.

> There is nothing worse than a young person having a great idea that fails because of a lack of coherent explanation. It does the young person's confidence no good, and it may be the last time they suggest anything for quite a while.

The dynamic of this format means that as well as focusing on the centre, people are forced through a pain barrier to admit before each other that they are worshipping. There is nowhere to hide. It has a massive impact on the levels of intimacy within a group that previously worshipped in their own private worlds when they take the plunge and say, 'Yes, I'm a Christian too, and I'm prepared to put wholehearted worship above my street cred.' Sometimes just a few people experiencing a release to truly express themselves in worship acts as a release mechanism for everyone else. The song 'Jesus, be the Centre' is an obvious choice for this arrangement.

What would our corporate worship physically look like if we were trying to create community rather than destroy it? How would things look if we wanted people to interact with the message? How would things look if we wanted everyone to have an opportunity to share their story and give a human face to our message?
John Albiston, www.phuture.org

Are we getting through?
Having an inspired idea from God is one thing for a young person, but explaining it to a group of other young people is something else much harder altogether. This is due to their attitudes (often subconscious) to communication. For many young people that I work with, communication has occurred if the words have escaped from their mouth in the right order at the right time. In their mind that is job done, task completed. It's a huge mindshift from that attitude to one where communication has not occurred until you know the recipients have heard and understood what you are attempting to communicate.

Simple communication skills are all it takes to get an idea across – most commonly absent are these.
  ◉ Having patience and assuming authority to ask everyone to be quiet

- Doing this in a calm, non-confrontational way
- Waiting until everyone is actually quiet before speaking
- Then speaking clearly and slowly, so that everyone has a chance to understand
- Repeating the statement so people can take on board both the 'how' and 'why' of what you are asking them to do
- Repeating things while the exercise is taking place to reinforce the key points, or stretch people on to a further thought
- Ending things well, with feedback, summary or explanation.

Training and empowering in this sort of presentational work is very important as there is nothing worse than a young person having a great idea that fails because of a lack of coherent explanation. It does the young person's confidence no good, and it may be the last time they suggest anything for quite a while. Another negative scenario is that they get gazumped by the leader, who comes up to explain properly after the young person has made a less-than-perfect job of it. 'What John was trying to say was… '. Any authority you conferred has just been snatched back.

Gently encouraging folks to step into authority by using simple skills like these makes them realise that it isn't a case of 'you've either got it or you haven't'. Given that stark choice, many young people assume they haven't got it.

Chapter 20

Band Interaction

Communication between the members of a young worship team is absolutely essential. There are some simple disciplines that, if you can instil them, go a long way to enabling young worshippers to develop into servants rather than stars. Trust and interdependence are key if giftings are to flourish and not be stifled.

We have all known the frustration of following a leader who is lost in wonder, love and praise but seemingly doesn't care

- ◉ whether anyone else is, or
- ◉ if anyone else in the team has something to offer, or
- ◉ if anyone else knows what he/she is going to do next.

I have been there. I've been that uncommunicative so and so who regarded it as appalling that my bass player was so out of touch with the Lord that he didn't realise I was going to repeat the fourth verse for the third time.

Everyone should have a chance to feed into the flow of the music. There is a difference between leading and controlling. As a leader, often you have to leave space to let other musicians take more of a lead. It should be said that the key communication in most band settings is that between the leader and the drummer. On this axis sits everything else.

Obviously it's hard to communicate verbally while singing, so a lot of leaders use signals to interact with their team. Whether you are using signals or not, it is essential that everyone in a team can see each other. Some people will not use signals but rely on following the style, speed, rhythm and volume of the leader's playing. The main problems with this are that

- ◉ often the sound is not of a high enough quality for everyone in the band to hear clearly what the leader is doing, and

◉ there are obvious constraints for those who want to lead without an instrument.

I'll let you into my strange little world of signals that permanently entertain the folks who regularly have to put up with playing with me.

[Increase volume/intensity]
When I feel that this should happen, I stomp my right heel to the ground. The harder I'm stomping, the louder I'm thinking. Sometimes, if things have been quiet for a while, a mild touch of the right foot lets the drummer know that I would love a little bit of rhythm to return.

[Decrease Volume/Intensity]
The opposite of the above is me opening my stance (apologies to the non-cricket-lovers among you). This is basically me angling my right foot towards two o'clock, though sometimes I have to get all the way to three o'clock before anyone notices. Inevitably your body twists when your foot leads.

[Cut all Music]
This usually happens at the end of a chord, so my hand just continues off my guitar and makes a sideways karate-like chop to the right.

[Tempo]
If I am wanting to decrease or increase the tempo, I stamp my left foot accordingly. I stamp faster than the present tempo to suggest a faster tempo and vice versa. This is especially useful for songs that end by slowing down.

[Let Me Take It]
If I want to drastically change the feel or the tempo, and need to be left on my own to do so, then I'll poke out my tongue (just a little!) in the general direction of whoever may need to stop playing so rhythmically. It basically means, 'Keep playing, but don't play anything that will control the tempo.'

[Bass and Drums]

If I want a classic bass and drums only section in a song, I will point my second and third fingers like a fork in their direction (horizontally, not vertically).

> There is nothing special about my signals, and I'm sure you can come up with a thousand better ones, but whatever you do make sure that everyone is watching and supporting the leader as much as possible, as he/she is attempting to communicate in three directions at once.

Chapter 21

Loops

Changing musical style is dependent on one thing above all others – rhythm. It is the biggest factor in what decides whether you call a track garage, trance or country.

In the last few years we have seen exponential growth in the rate of rhythm change. Whereas rock 'n' roll was the pre-eminent style for almost ten years, nowadays we're lucky if a style stays 'in' for more than six months such is the speed of change.

So it's understandable that youth workers and musicians feel that it's impossible to stay relevant, especially when the new rhythms require a high level of drumming expertise. The rhythms behind dance (and much pop) material are programmed via samplers and sequencers (music-based computers) which can play any drum in any order at breakneck speed, often leaving the rhythm outside the physical capabilities of a human drummer.

This is one of the reasons that in the last five or six years we have being using sampled loops in worship. These are short (mostly four bars) sections of rhythm that have either been electronically created or are recordings of live drummers forced through a raft of effects to give them a bit of an 'edge'. These sections then loop continuously to provide the backbone of a track.

Dependent on the type of loop, they can give drummers the freedom to play on top of it (to give added dynamics), or render a drummer unnecessary (which can also sometimes be useful). This is the kind of stuff you really want to let your decks-friendly and computer-savvy young people get stuck into. The software for playing and downloading these loops is readily available on the web (see www.youthwork.co.uk/resources/ for links), and once you have some you are happy with simply burn 10 minutes worth of each loop onto CD for use in a live worship setting. The beauty is that they work alongside an acoustic guitar for 15 people or with a full band for larger crowds.

We really do miss out on interacting with young people's souls (as well as their minds and spirits) unless rhythm connects to their guts. For example, as an Irishman I find there is something that extra bit special when I'm singing a worship song with an Irish feel. As well as connecting with my mind and spirit, it is connecting with something deep inside. It is connecting with a large part of what makes me, me. I have seen many young people released into worship and movement because they felt loops like this in their gut.

Loops are a simple way of encouraging people to start rapping and MC-ing without someone else having to beatbox for half an hour. The loops quickly reproduce rap-friendly hip-hop grooves more easily than a drummer will.

[Points to remember]

When using a loop the most important thing is to make sure that everyone can hear it, otherwise everything falls apart pretty quickly. This is especially true for a drummer, who may want to listen to the track in headphones.

If you don't have a DJ you could create a new band member who is on 'hardware'. This means that with a signal from whoever is leading, the loop can fade up or fade down sensitively, avoiding surreal starts and stops. If you have someone with DJ equipment, the feel of the loop can be manipulated by some simple use of EQ and filters.

All the information you need to get going and two free loops are there on www.youthwork.co.uk/resources/.

Don't get freaked by the technology side of this. It really isn't too taxing. If needs be, delegate.

Chapter 22

Dynamics

What is happening in the modern 'worship experience'? I should start out by saying that I don't write as a cynical observer, but as a practitioner of the modern worship experience in many of its forms from small groups of four to crowds of four thousand or more.

Understanding the dynamics of worship is especially critical in our work with young people, as otherwise we lay ourselves open to allegations of manipulation and exploitation.

> Jesus was the ultimate charismatic leader, so I don't think we should be scared of this stuff. We simply need to be responsible with the enormous power that is handed to us in leading young people in worship.

Take the example of a youth group of twenty young people going to an event in a nearby town for a thousand young people. Everyone has a fantastic time. On the way home we may casually say, 'The worship was so much better tonight. God really showed up.' But perhaps an outside observer could also give this analysis.

- Everyone had higher levels of expectation and excitement, because you travelled to a different venue and the event only happens four times per year.
- There was a concentration of musical talent, because of the larger pool to draw from, so the band was much more impressive.
- The large numbers created a positive feedback loop of learned behaviour and emotion, such as the initiation of clapping or hand raising.
- A positive feedback loop is also one of the precursors for disinhibited hysterical behaviour; such as crying and uttering meaningless words.

- ◎ The volume of singing was fifty times louder and the intensity of the silence was more significant because more people were silent.
- ◎ There was the excitement of learning new songs, giving a buzz of discovery.
- ◎ The larger numbers meant a professional sound and lighting rig was used, which made everything look and sound impressive.
- ◎ The evening was presented by 'cool' people on a raised stage, which conferred some authority on them.
- ◎ A charismatic leader was 'imported' for the event, and he used classic communication and crowd control skills.
- ◎ There was an element of freedom involved in being away from your normal circumstances, and freedom in your anonymity in a large crowd, enhancing your ability to let go.

Crowd dynamics are natural and God-created, and I am in no way suggesting that if something has a natural explanation then it isn't God-given as a means of encouragement and community. But there is a fine line between using a natural force and relying on it. I have spent much time discussing the dynamics of Christian gatherings with unbelieving psychiatrists, who happily attribute every experience to positive feedback loops of affirmation and belief.

[How long does this exhilaration last, and what impact does it have on the moment-by-moment choices of life?]

I suppose at times I would say, 'I agree, but is that a problem?'

There is a biblical pattern for festivals and journeys. God loves the great spectacle as well as the still, small voice. The fact is that God uses gatherings to build faith in his people through each other. It is useful to note, however, that if we aren't careful how we describe God at work we may create later disappointment. We may well make it seem that God is impotent when he apparently does not do the things in a small group setting that he did in the larger setting. If we saw more clearly what was going on we might have the freedom to say that God was in fact at work through the intricacies of how he created us with our need of encouragement, our desire to be together, faith that rises when both are combined in large numbers, and the Holy Spirit blowing powerfully where he wills to convict, comfort and challenge people. Wonderfully there are times that God moves in a supernatural way that no one can explain, even though sceptics often try.

Jesus was the ultimate charismatic leader, so I don't think we should be scared of this stuff. We simply need to be responsible with the enormous power that is handed to us in leading young people in worship and perhaps we do need to acknowledge that at times the impact of a leader may be a function of their 'charisma' (in the secular sense) as much as their anointing.

Keeping these things in mind at least lets us keep an eye out for unhelpful assumptions, which may arise in young people, and lets us allow smaller gatherings to be small. This breeds a state where we stop seeking a big experience in the midst of a small gathering, thus missing the beautiful and distinct possibilities of a small gathering that a large one does not so easily provide.

The ten dynamics listed earlier cannot be lazily explained away as spiritual, because the same dynamics occur in many other settings. At a football match for instance.

There is a phenomenal feeling of togetherness with the fans of one's own side. People we have never met before suddenly become deserving of hugs, kisses and manly slaps on the back. Emotions that would not rise so strongly in us when alone are magnified perhaps ten-fold. Anger that would not normally show its face, or tears of joy that would usually be hidden from public gaze, form a river with the other springs around us. Common purpose is being shared and our feelings, thoughts, prejudices and beliefs are being strongly reinforced by all those around us. We leave the ground potentially exhilarated by what we have experienced. However, how long does this exhilaration last, and what impact does it have on the moment-by-moment choices of life?

Does any of this sound familiar?

Departure

Some of the people I was involved in leading worship with as a teenager and student don't worship God any more. A few of them genuinely believe we were deluding ourselves.

It causes me to ask serious questions about our shared worship experiences. Did we take enough care to ensure it was actually God involved, and that we hadn't been swept away by waves of peer pressure and emotion as they now believe? How much of what we experienced was a nineties version of community singing, which held people together, gave them a shared purpose, and fed their aspirations for a better life? Were we just a Christianised version of a mining town's brass band?

Does our worship have enough cultural relevance to retain any meaning when someone encounters the bright lights of university or the freedom of having money and a job? Will worship then feel like a separate reality from a shadow world, or a present reality that interacts with the here-and-now world? Do we give people the space to bring their doubts to worship, or do our 'production-line' formulas constrain them to the beaten track?

> The inadequacies in the way we worship God don't change the truth that he is worth worshipping.

Surely it is better to be able to express doubts and work through them in the teenage years amongst a supportive group with some older wisdom, than to wait until we crash on our own a few years later. If we force young people to sing only the words we give them, we may never know where they really stand.

I don't have an answer for many of these questions, but I know two things for definite.

One. What happened to my mates is not rare. I have seen it replicated and heard similar stories from youth workers and church leaders all over the UK. The drop-off rate of our young people is appalling. I know there are many factors at play in this, and I am not trying to lay all the blame at worship's door, but something that had so much to do with bringing people in has to share some of the responsibility when they accuse it of being a fraud and their reason for getting out.

Two. God hasn't changed. He is still there, immovable and majestic. My belief that he is true, which is at the root of my worship, has not changed one iota. The inadequacies in the way we worship God don't change the truth that he is worth worshipping.

IDEAS
ideas
Ideas for

Distinctive Worship
ideas

ideas
ideas

Distinctive Worship
ideas

Criteria

Before we get into the Ideas Section, these are the criteria we have in mind when developing worship for young people. It should make use of:

[Interaction]
Whereby not everything that happens is prescribed from the front. Where everyone feels that they can have an impact on the direction of a session. Where conscious decisions have to be made to engage in a certain activity.

[Individual Creativity]
Where space is created for individuals to respond to God in a way that expresses something of who they are, as opposed to slavishly following the lowest common denominator option. This may be through drawing, painting, writing, dancing, or any number of creative media.

[Communal Aspect]
Where actions, words and structures reinforce the importance of community worshipping together.

[Use of Visual Media]
Where still images (paper/screen) or moving images (DVD/video/animation) provide stimulation and reinforcement for certain themes.

[Earthed Experiences]
Where the context and content of a session can be referenced to real-life experiences of a young person's week, enabling resonance with spiritual and physical reality.

[Musical Accessibility]

Where the musical styles used correspond with young people's understood musical lexicon, rather than creating a separate genre that runs the risk of making God seem irrelevant, as its musicality becomes irrelevant.

And with songs we're looking at those

- That make use of modern imagery (but not necessarily exclusively)
- That have strong thematic 'hooks'
- That are theologically sound
- That use modern language
- That use modern physical movements.

Introduction

You'll spot very quickly that none of this is rocket science. All it takes is a bit of praying, and opening your mind to think a little more laterally. The ideas here are intended to pull the tent pegs of your head a bit wider, to release your own creativity.

[General Thoughts]

- ◉ Some of the ideas involve shouting or writing names for God, or words to describe God. This is sometimes a struggle for those who cannot just pluck words from the air. One way of helping is by reading a story about Jesus, and encouraging folks to shout words describing how Jesus was in the story, e.g. caring, brave, gentle, peaceful, powerful.
- ◉ Another angle from reading a passage is encouraging folks to pick one person from the passage, then think themselves into their shoes. They can enter in to why that person would be worshipping.
- ◉ Encourage the young people to bring Bibles for worship and to participate by reading passages or verses in the midst of the music. Perhaps kick-start the process somewhat by giving some young people specific verses to read, but let them decide when to speak them out.
- ◉ Encourage people to shout 'amen' or 'yes' or whatever they want in response to what other people read or pray. It keeps everyone participating, awake and focused on the fact that they are worshipping and not watching a performance.
- ◉ Make space for folks to share testimonies in the midst of worship, both to thank God for what he has done and to encourage those listening. Nurturing some of these into songs can be very powerful.
- ◉ Don't be afraid of space and silence.

The ideas are split into five, which roughly represent six areas of interaction.

Hands:	things we create or shape
Feats:	things we do or experience
Mouths:	things we say or sing
Eyes and Ears:	things we see or hear
Fingers:	things we write or draw

OT stands for Original Thought, and indicates the person whose original thought the idea is based on. Many thanks to you all for your creative sparks.

Hands

[Museum Takeaway]

One or two weeks before the event, ask everyone to create a piece of art that expresses something about God or how they feel about God. If people need further focus, give them a theme. The piece could be a painting, a photo, a sculpture, a computer presentation or a recording. Explain beforehand that every piece on display will be taken home by someone else, so no one gets upset when it happens.

Arrange for these pieces to be collected or dropped off before everyone arrives.

On the night, display them anonymously all over the venue. Go to town on the presentation of the items: firstly to give it a professional museum feel, so folks stop properly and examine each piece, and secondly to confer value on the artistic efforts of the young people. Lighting, framing, titling and positioning will all be important.

On arrival, as the curator of the museum give a short introduction that builds up the exhibits. Explain that there will be a period of time when they can wander through all the exhibits, but encourage folks to pray that God would speak to them through what they see, hear or touch and that they would be inspired by each other's art into worship. Let everyone generally mill around, but make it clear that the point is to spend a decent length of time, probably seated, in front of maybe one or two exhibits that really catch the eye or ear, rather than just race around them all.

There is a buzz derived from desiring to know who has created what. After a length of time explain that if someone wants to take home a specific piece they now need to discover who the artist is and get them to explain the story behind it (having first shared what they themselves see in it). Obviously in the process of trying to find your artist, you have the experience of hearing many of the other stories from the other artists that you try along the way. It becomes a large mass of explanation, conversation and worship.

[Graffiti Worship Walls]

These have been great successes all over of the country, especially in the context of 24-7 prayer rooms. Folks who would never pray out loud will pray using paint and pencil. Many youth workers testify to their amazement at the spiritual depth of the worship and prayers of their teenagers when given the space to creatively express themselves. Walls very quickly become filled with prayer requests or worship based on photos, magazine articles or newspaper clippings that have also been stuck there. It creates a very real sense of community and ministering to one another, as there is a gradual build-up of material that speaks to the next people to be there. The wall can be running in conjunction with a sung worship session, where both are feeding into the flow of each other. You can get more help and information on setting up walls and rooms from www.24-7prayer.com.

Needless to say, your worship walls don't have to be walls. There are any number of creative ways to make a blank canvas for potential scribblers. I have seen lining paper wrapped around church architecture in many ways.

[Help me Hold on] – (*Distinctive Sounds* – ICC)

This song is based on the memorable concepts of 'stashing' and 'trashing'. Ask God to show you the things in your life that need to disappear, and the things that need to be held on to. Bins and treasure chests are the perfect receptacles.

Get folks to scribble the things to stash, and the things to trash, on separate bits of paper and then deposit them in the appropriate receptacle during the song. You could provide lots of examples (e.g. unhealthy late-night television, patience, dodgy jokes, encouragement) on pieces of paper all over the floor that folks must then lift and decide where they are putting them. Explain that the decision is with regard to their lives, and not just a bland decision on whether something is good or bad.

With some preparation, this can also be done with actual items. There may well be some things that it would be good for folks to get rid of. Make sure they also bring things that they are resolving to 'stash' and give more priority to – e.g. Bible, letters to friends/relatives etc.

You could also have a 'stashing' list and a 'trashing' list on opposite sides of a room, or on two screens. As people continually add to these during the course of the song, folks will be encouraged and challenged by each other's choices.

[Gift Giving]

Explain that we worship God when we offer back to him the gifts and talents that he has given to us. Read the story of the feeding of the five thousand from John 6. Explain how what may seem like a pathetic amount of stuff to us – a very small talent, a potential dream, an ability to do something that no one else likes doing – can be multiplied by God into something literally miraculous. Use a song such as 'All I Am' (Andy Flannagan, *SON*, ICC79530).

1) Give everyone a blank acetate, and get folks to scribble their gifts and talents in different colours on their particular sheet. Then as people feel able to give their gifts back to God during the course of the song, they can lay down their sheet on the OHP. There is a layering effect, which is really powerful, as folks see their gifts joined with the gifts of others in the body.

2) Ask people to write down on sheets of paper the things they are good at. During the song, scrunch up the pieces of paper and place them on an OHP screen until it is totally filled with everyone's gifts. Look at them and think about how effective the body could be if we brought all our gifts together like this.

3) Warn folks a week before the event, asking them to bring an item that represents what they believe God is leading them into or gifting them with. Wrap some wire netting into hammock-like constructions where these can be laid and displayed during worship. As people mingle, encourage them to try to link an object to its owner, and if necessary do some detective work to find out the story behind certain items. This is often the first time that some will have discovered each other's dreams and passions. Encourage folks to then pray together and ask for full release of God's gifting to each other.

[Stones]

Basically everybody gets a fist-sized stone. This is an especially useful exercise if you are on retreat by the sea, as the process of going to find and select your own stone makes the whole thing more memorable.

Once each of them has a stone, tell them to feel its contours and look at its colours. Wonder at the fact that there is no other stone like it. It is completely unique. Just like them.

Read the passage from Joshua 4 where the Israelites used stones from the Jordan to remind them of God's amazing acts on their behalf.

Get them to use a felt-tip pen and write short phrases on the stone that remind them of times in their life when God has 'come through' or made himself very real to them. Tell them to try thinking through the different people, places and events that have been significant in their life.

They can share these moments with the group, or just give thanks to God in prayer for these times. You may well be surprised at how much you've forgotten (I certainly was!). It is a good lesson in not taking God for granted.

Link the stone's uniqueness to these acts as well. God has done all these things for you and only you. Marvel at how he has moved differently in everyone's life.

Invite them to keep the stone in a prominent place (on a desk, or by the television) where it can act as a permanent reminder of God's intervention in their life.

[Snap Art]

Spread out rolls of paper on the floor or walls for folks to paint and draw on. Usually it is better for this to be themed, as otherwise it can just become playschool! Poster paints and chalks seem to be the most useful weapons.

This can be an exercise in itself, or an option during sung worship. Either way, it is good to give strong visual or verbal stimuli to kick off the creative juices. The stimuli could continue during the exercise, via a CD track or sections of the Bible being read.

It works well to take digital photos of the works of art and upload them into a slide show, so individual worship can be shared and appreciated by everyone. This has the advantage of enabling you to email people shots of their work. You can suggest that people use it as their PC desktop.

Rolls of paper with felt pens spread out on the floor can be great for increasing the extent to which everyone is ministering to each other. We have experienced some powerful times when people share in writing what they feel God is saying to the group, or just share their personal prayers. Gradually as people write, then read, then wander around the room, then write more because they are inspired by what they have read, there is a real sense of a positive feedback loop. Folk are sticking their necks out to encourage, challenge and prophesy as they worship.

[Verse Posters]

Create a poster based on a Bible verse that expresses worship to God.

Spread many Bibles and much artwork equipment around a floor. Then encourage folks to pray before diving into their creativity. You may need to be on hand quite a lot to provide help in finding where favourite verses, or certain types of verses, are in the Bible. (This might be a good chance to introduce them to concordances or a Bible CD-ROM with quick search facilities.) Their poster could contain the actual words of the verse, or just reflect the spirit of the verse. Display all the posters in a gallery and encourage people to explain their drawings to each other.

[Snap-happy]

With the advent of very cheap (and often free) low resolution digital cameras it should be feasible for nearly anyone to make an almost instant slide show based on photos that folks have just taken. See www.irfanview.com for slide show software (easier and faster than MS PowerPoint).

Basically during the first half of an evening (preferably in summer) send folks out in twos or threes with a camera to get creative on a certain theme such as people, creativity, colour, death, the church, sin – just use your imagination.

You can use these as a slide show in the second half of an evening with an appropriate track or worship song. Sometimes bringing the outside world into the building is no bad thing. It can give a very real edge to the worship and prayer.

[Washed in the River]

Get a long, wide roll of blue paper. Unroll it down the centre of the space you are using. It is – surprise, surprise – a river. Read Hebrews 10:19–22 about having our bodies washed with pure water.

(There are some powerful images of people cleansing themselves in rivers on the DVD *1Giant Leap* and the CD-ROM *Living Water* on highwayvideo.com's Vibe1.) Explain that only through his sacrifice does Jesus wash us clean. Encourage folks from either side of the river to come down to its edge and be 'washed' in it. They can kneel and/or symbolically place their hands in the stream while praying prayers of repentance or singing a song like 'Wash me Clean'.

Use painting pencils to write down the sins you want to be washed away. Someone can then brush them into a stream of colour, taking them away down the river.

Of course, if you have a hygienic local river to hand (we don't in Luton) then you may want to use that instead.

[At the Foot of the Cross]
Find or make a large wooden cross.

Get people to kneel at the foot of the cross and encourage them to speak privately to God, asking him to take their worries, sins and burdens. Read Colossians 2:13–14, which finishes with the words 'nailing it to the cross'.

Use the track 'At the Foot of the Cross' by 100 hours (*Spring Harvest New Songs 2002*).

Get folks to write the things they prayed about on paper and then pin this like the written code to the cross.

Ask people to intentionally move away after they have prayed, leaving what they have written with God.

[Signing]
Get a trained person to teach the group some sign language for your most frequently used songs. This often really helps those who find it hard to express themselves verbally or in any other way. There is a beauty to this form of expression that also ministers extensively to those watching, as well as the obvious benefits for hearing impaired young people. One session may even provide the stimulus for a member of the group to consider enrolling in a course.

[Sea Of Hands]
A simple but very fun concept – passing people around on a sea of hands (crowd surfing) while thanking God for them. In effect you are using that person as your raw material for worship. Make sure everyone gets a turn. At times you may want to quite literally just

hold the person up in prayer. One person singing out thanks with one instrument can help alongside this.

OT: Tim Hewitt

[Pass The Parcel]

Picture the scene – everyone is passing around a parcel, while singing their lungs out or dancing their legs off, but suddenly the worship band or CD stops. Each layer of wrapping has a worship suggestion instead of a forfeit.

Make it clear that these are for everyone to do, even if the unwrapper gets to direct proceedings somewhat. Example ideas are; 'Pick one person to thank God for', 'Tell one story from this week where you were aware of God', 'Pick one thing that makes you love God'. Everyone else echoes with words of worship, before the band or the worship track kicks off again.

OT: Jude Smith

[It Only Takes A Candle…]

This can give a powerful extra dimension to the many songs with light as a central theme, especially if there is a mission theme to an event. Give everyone a candle, then turn all the lights off. Light just one candle at one spot in the room, then watch as that candle lights another candle, which lights another, and there is a staggeringly quick spread around the room. It's a potent reminder of how fast things could change.

Read Matthew 5:14–16 during this.

[Rhythmic rotation]

While sitting in a circle, start a rhythm using clapping, slapping and clicking. Everyone then has to shout in time with the rhythm one reason to praise God. Just keep going until you're out of ideas or on the floor.

OT: Jude Smith

[Stained glass prayers]

If you have a window that light streams through, then an effective exercise is to create a stained glass window of prayers and thanks.

Provide crepe or other suitably thin paper that can be creatively chopped up by the young people. Then write prayers to God on those pieces of paper that have sprung out of the context of your worship, and stick them on to the window. It's inspiring to look at the effect when the light breaks through, as it is a powerful visual symbol of God working on our prayers.

A variation on this theme is assembling a collage of world headlines, and then using the light streaming through these as a picture of how God shines his light into these situations.

[Gallery]

Create a programmed route or enable random journeying around various points in a room where you have arranged pieces of pottery, sculpture, pictures, photos etc alongside questions or suggestions for response and action. The first question should be as open as possible, as the same piece of art may well mean completely different things to different people.

e.g. Rembrandt's *Return of the Prodigal Son*

Q: What do you think is going on here?

Q: Look at the scene. Identify who you think is the father, the younger son, the older son, and the mother.

Read the story from Luke chapter 15.

Q: From each of these perspectives, write down what you would want to say to the other characters in the story.

Q: Let these new perspectives on God as Father lead you into expressing some personal worship to him.

[Jenga]

If you can cope with the sacrilege of writing on your precious blocks, then this activity certainly holds attention. Scribble simple worship suggestions on each block (thank God for his power, thank God that he is a healer, and so on). When you pull that block out just do what it says. The loser has to sing Psalm 119.

OT: Jude Smith

[Ball games]

Grab a ball and throw it randomly at anyone standing in a circle. On catching the ball they have to shout something that they are thankful for, then chuck it at the next victim. Encourage everyone to listen to each other's suggestions and let that build up a larger range of things to be thankful for in their own lives. If you're anything like me, you'll come up with the same three things again and again. Let's widen our worship vocabulary. A ball hurtling towards you can be surprisingly helpful in stimulating this.

OT: Tim Hewitt

[Worries Bin]

Take some time to think about the things that worry you. If it helps, break your thinking down into sections such as school, home, friends, relationships, future. In each of the sections scribble these worries down onto a piece of paper, then leave them with God. Read or display Matthew 6:25–34. To symbolise the fact that you are leaving these worries behind, one by one, scrumple them up and throw them in the bin. Encourage folks to keep doing this mentally and physically when worries and anxiety return. Don't promise a quick fix.

You could sing the verses that end that passage to finish. 'Seek ye First' – a fantastic long forgotten song – works really well as a punk rock epic in D (just try it, you'll see what I mean). Include lots of pogo-ing and shout '2,3,4' just before the chorus.

OT: Eden – YFC Gillingham

IDEAS

Feats

This is another good way of 'earthing' worship into people's normal lives. This is obviously best done with a small group in a house, but can also be reproduced with a lot of fun on a bigger scale (with some preparation) in a hall.

The premise is to spend 10 minutes or so in each room of the house, and to focus on how we worship God in doing what we do there. Don't just talk about these things – do them for a few moments and just be aware of God being there.

Some examples:

Bathroom – When we look in the mirror, do we feel worshipful? Can we look at other parts of creation and be thankful, but not for what we see here? Do we worry more about man who looks on the outward appearance or the Lord who looks at the heart? Do we feel clean when we come to God in worship? What if every time we had a shower we asked for God's forgiveness to wash us clean of our sins?

Bedroom – Do we get enough sleep? Are we alive enough to God when we wake up? Can we invite God to be part of our dreams? Bring to God as worship all the other things that you do there – homework, video games, surfing the net, reading, listening to music. How can each of these be worship? Proverbs 3:6, 'In all your ways acknowledge him, and he will make your paths straight.'

This may also be an appropriate time to pray in repentance for selfishness and unhealthy reading, viewing or surfing.

Living room – What we truly worship is decided by what we spend most of our time doing. Have a think about how many hours a day you watch TV. How can we give our relaxation time to God? Do we make an effort to worship God with the other people in our houses, if we can? What about every time we use a remote control, we wonder who's actually in control of us?

Kitchen – When was the last time we worshipped by serving the other people in our house; cooking, doing the dishes, or cleaning some surfaces. Are we aware when we are creating a meal of echoing God's creativity? Is that why it brings us pleasure? How thankful are we for the food that we have and enjoy?

[Musical Prayers]

Cover sheets of A4 paper with separate worship suggestions (e.g. shout a name for God three times, thank God for your best mate, sing one chorus of a song, be silent for 30 seconds) and spread them over the floor. Play bouncing loud music – everyone bounces around manically from square to square on the floor until – you guessed it – the music stops and they have to follow the instructions. A colourful patchwork of sheets looks fun and inviting when spread all over the floor. As I participated in this activity and watched young people do the same it was one of those times when the personal and the corporate splurged together in one happy moving mass. People are released into their own worship by the encouragement of the noise all around them.

Other suggestions for the sheets.

- Shout out one thing you are grateful for
- Stop, ask God what he wants to say
- Tell God one thing you love about him
- Tell God about your day
- Ask God for something you want
- Ask God for something for one of your friends
- Shout out the name of someone you want to become a Christian
- Thank God for one person in your life
- Tell God something you want forgiveness for
- Tell God someone you want to forgive

Things like the above list of suggestions could be used in many contexts. Let your mind run wild. They could be in crackers, or on different blackboards in different classrooms.

OT: Jude Smith

[Zones]

In the context of a celebration, it is often helpful to have different zones where people can participate in very different expressions of worship. Prepare a leader for each zone, or very clear instructions on printed cards. What often works best is to make some sort of loud noise (like banging a cymbal) every 15 minutes to get folks to change to the next zone.

Example zones are:

Foot Washing

Read the story of Jesus' amazing act from John 13. Underline how it was even more amazing because of the context of his imminent betrayal. Spread a few bowls and towels around the room. Be aware of the dynamics of your group (e.g. keeping guys and girls separate), and be prepared to lead by example.

There are many talking points that spring from the experience. How did it feel to have a friend washing your feet? How did it feel to do the washing? What similar simple tasks of service can we do for our friends and family? Why were we comfortable with certain people doing it, but not others?

Silence

See example on page 58.

Writing a postcard to God

If you can find postcards that represent your locality all the better, as this will make the exercise that little bit more real. This is a good discipline for concisely telling God how you are feeling and how you feel about him. The size of a postcard is less intimidating to younger teenagers. It's probably useful to have a mock postbox constructed so the cards do physically go somewhere. (Make it clear that you will not be reading them!) Folks may want to claim them back later, to keep as a staging post on their journey with God.

Map of the world

Find the largest map of the world you can. Alternatively trace continent outlines onto a blank acetate, then project it onto a wall. Leave this visible during the whole of the session.

Get hold of video material such as Tearfund's 'Art for Mercy' video (www.artformercy.org.uk) and use it to explain how when we worship, we worship with our brothers and sisters across the world. You could use post-it notes to stick prayers for various countries to their appropriate spot on the map and rejoice that God is God of the whole world, perhaps using songs like 'Over all the Earth'.

Town tour

A great example of what can be achieved with a bit of holistic and lateral thinking is what some of the young people of south Luton got up to.

Each week the group was taken to a significant spot in the town as a discussion starter and as a precursor to worship. They went to Luton F.C. ground – does everyone worship? The magistrates' court – does God care about justice? Vauxhall car plant – what can we worship? Luton cemetery – worship eternal. Luton airport – who are we worshipping with? The top of the multi-storey car park – what is God's perspective? The golf course – the discipline of worship? The town hall – the Holy Spirit and power. A squeezed down version of this could be done in one evening as a kind of whistle stop tour.

This also provides opportunities to speak into the significance of spiritual warfare, with worship as a powerful weapon in changing the spiritual temperature of a town.

Your own local areas will have their own points of interest, I'm sure.

OT: Dave Steell

[Uncomfortable]

There is an amazing passage at the end of 2 Samuel where David is in trouble with God for not being obedient in maintaining his army. God has sent a plague upon Israel, but has stopped at Jerusalem on condition that David builds an altar to him. So under instructions through Gad the prophet, David makes his way to the threshing-floor of Araunah. Araunah is more than willing to provide the raw materials for the altar, as you can see.

> *Araunah said to David, "Let my lord the king take whatever pleases him and offer it up. Here are oxen for the burnt offering, and here are threshing-sledges and ox yokes for the wood. O king, Araunah gives all this to the*

king." Araunah also said to him, "May the LORD your God accept you."

In a time of crisis, surely this is a most helpful act of generosity, but David says something that took my breath away the first time I read it.

But the king replied to Araunah, "No, I insist on paying you for it. I will not sacrifice to the LORD my God burnt offerings that cost me nothing."

2 Samuel 24:22–23

David was saying that he wanted his worship of the Sovereign Lord to make a mark on him. He didn't want it to be free, or easy.

So often I will ask certain questions of people as they come to worship. Are we prepared for our worship of God to cost us something? To cost us in terms of our respectability, to cost us in terms of our comfort, or to cost us in terms of our enjoyment?

Are we prepared to worship in a way that is outside our comfort zones, so that we too can say, 'I will not sacrifice to the Lord my God burnt offerings that cost me nothing'?

If folks are usually sitting down, perhaps they should be jumping around. If they are always jumping around, perhaps they should be on their faces. If they are always the ones shouting out loud prayers, perhaps they should be silent. And if they are usually meek and mild, perhaps it is time to lead everyone in a loud praise shout.

The musicians may need to be far from any noise, and those who don't usually play perhaps need to make a joyful noise. Do you see where I'm going? Times like this have seen people released from inhibitions and have corrected some attitudes (especially in me) that worship should always feel nice. As I was leading one of these times, I faced a personal struggle of leaving my guitar in its case. For me, I guess that is my 'default mode' for worship. It was really hard to resist the temptation to grab the guitar to finish things off nicely in a safe way. I had to experience a bit of cost to how I wanted things done, and sing without my security blanket. The first time we did this, I failed; but the next time I managed it! I sometimes hate it when you have to lead by example.

The fabulous footnote to the Samuel story is that Araunah's threshing floor is the spot where Solomon eventually builds the temple. David's obedience became the foundation for worship for generations.

[Goaaalllllll!]

One thing that always seems to free young people up to get active in worship is to take them back to where they were when Beckham was stepping up to take 'that penalty' against Argentina. By this stage the boys and the girls are both listening. I ask them to remember where they were sitting, and then remember what they did at the moment the ball hit the back of the net. Much vertical leaping took place all over England at that moment I suspect.

The point is easily made that if it is worth getting vertically excited about a human being putting a blown-up bit of leather in the back of a net, it's worth getting even more excited about what the maker of the whole universe has done for us. It connects with that feeling and experience, and frees people to bounce for appropriate tracks.

[Random Acts Of Kindness]

Two good friends of mine love to bless and surprise the car behind them at the Dartford crossing by paying their toll.

Encourage your group to think about who could benefit from a random act of kindness. This may be someone within the group, or someone that no one knows; the homeless guy who needs a meal, the sad lady who would just love some flowers, or the old man whose car needs washing but he can't bend down any more. Send folks off to later return and share stories, or set the random act as a challenge for the upcoming week.

OT: Tim Hewitt

[Stop By A Window]

Send the members of the group outside to stop in one spot for 15 minutes and just be. Their job is to look for 'windows' through which to see God. Some will look at how the clouds move, some at the traffic, and some at the complexity of a tree or an animal. Everyone then returns and shares what they 'saw' through the window. The discipline here is actually being able to stay still in one place, noticing the things that you would not normally notice. Such as how many cars go past one point in a minute, how everyone walks in a similar way but looks completely different, how even the highest buildings don't reach the sky.

I have been amazed at the profound thoughts that young people return with. This exercise also makes an important point about God's presence and movement in all sectors of life. After times like this I am certainly more aware of God's presence in random moments, even in the most unlikely places. Just pondering on the complexity of any scene for long enough can fill you with amazement. I would only use this idea with older teenagers.

[Fasting]

This is not the easiest thing to get into for young people from a self-gratifying society. The key is to start small and focus on the reason for fasting, not the fasting itself. (Otherwise it starts to feel like a sponsored event!)

You could encourage suggestions from your young people of other regular activities from which they could fast. Underline that the choice to not partake in an activity is not just a religious thing but an act of worship, when it is done for the right reasons. I cannot think about this issue without laughing at the memory of Ardal O'Hanlon (Dougal from *Father Ted*) pontificating about our attitude to fasting as Christians. He said that while other religions and races didn't eat for whole months and denied themselves various types of meat, we had the whole thing nicely sorted. 'So, Seamus, what are you giving up for Lent?' 'Er, Em. Snickers.' What great sacrifices we make.

This is such a counter-cultural notion these days that you may well need to underline the biblical precedent for fasting and its key link to worship.

[Email]

Set up an email forum (very easy to do via yahoo.com or topica. com) whose sole purpose is for folks to offer up their thanks, and share the good and bad things that have been happening. Suggest that everyone types in the Bible verses that have spoken to them on a particular day. Again, positive feedback tends to kick in and community is shared.

Another idea is to get individuals to set up a 'god' hotmail address like god3427@hotmail.com. At the end of each day, they can use this for personal worship and prayer. For some people, this may actually be their most natural way of communicating with God. A nightly email is similar to a journal entry, except it shoots off into cyberspace. I don't know if God has an email account, but I do know that he definitely hears what we honestly express to him in whatever format.

[Worship Magpies]
Send everyone outside for a defined period of time with the mission of bringing back something that speaks to them of God and his way of doing things. Everyone then shares about what they have brought back. Some fun can be had by trying to guess the reasons why someone has picked a certain object. Stress the importance of not breaking any laws in obtaining the items.

OT: Tim Hewitt

[Selah]
There is a word in Psalms that many people skip over, probably due, ironically, to the fast pace of modern life. That word is 'selah'. Psalms has been enshrined as just another book in our flimsily-leafed Bibles for so long that we forget that Psalms is in fact a songbook.

Selah is not just a random word, but an instruction to the musicians and singers to stop or play instrumentally. It was designed as a natural pause for reflection on the words that had preceded it. Never has there been a bigger need for selah in the midst of our worship. In our desire to be musically coherent, often we flow through many songs in a whistle-stop tour that leaves no room to breathe or reflect.

If you want to get creative you could put a large pause sign on a screen. Often these pauses provide space for God to speak to individuals, which may lead to the session being taken in a new direction.

[Wow!!]
Encourage folks to be on the lookout for things that make them go 'wow!' Whether it is a new dance move in a music video, a moment of extreme kindness, a great view, or an amazing quote from a book, get them to bring something representing that moment to share it with everyone else at the end of the week. You could make the exercise a regular thing, so that folks are learning to look out for

anything transcendent in their everyday lives and learning to give God the glory for it. This is also a fabulous way of getting the young people to share something of what makes them tick. Folks will begin to identify with each other, and a little bit of community is built.

[You have Turned] – (*The Source*)

'You have Turned' is a great song that emphasises God's power to turn negative situations around, and the classic movement in the chorus of spinning (and jumping if you want) helps to solidify the concept.

You could do this simple exercise to emphasise the 180 degree nature of how God turns bad situations to good. On one wall you could get the young people to scribble up various negative situations that they have experienced. On the wall directly opposite, ask folks to scribble descriptions of how God turned the situation around. Then everyone has a chance to move from side to side and be encouraged by the stories.

During the song people can quite literally turn from the negative to the positive. You could have all the sheets on one side forming a massive minus sign, and the others forming a massive plus sign. Some folks may be writing about negative situations that haven't seen anything positive happening. In these cases, turning to face the other wall could be a powerful statement of faith, and way of speaking prophetically into the situation. Young people could encourage each other by scribbling up the positive outcomes that could occur in a situation, which the actual person involved cannot yet see. During the song, you could also get individuals to share verbal testimonies of how God has moved in a specific situation, to build faith in the others.

[Labyrinth]

The labyrinth is an interactive installation to enable spiritual journeys. It takes as its inspiration the labyrinths of medieval cathedrals, which symbolised the path of the soul through life. The contemporary version is a one-way maze taped out on the floor of a medium sized hall area.

Participants walk the labyrinth at their own pace wearing a CD player. Each track on the CD contains meditations, instructions and music relating to the 10 stages of the labyrinth where people take part in symbolic activities such as dropping a stone into water to represent 'letting go'. I cannot recommend it highly enough.

You can create your own labyrinth with the official starter pack available from YFC (with full instructions and CDs with the meditations and tracks) or purchase the online version on CD-ROM. Call 0121 550 8055 or email yfc@yfc.co.uk for information.

[Tabernacle]

One of the challenges with this age group is putting worship in its proper historical context, especially with regard to the Old Testament.

If you are feeling adventurous you could create the main facets of the Tabernacle in a hall, and allow everyone to go through the process of experiencing what the priests experienced. This brings some deeper understanding to some of the language we use in worship. Of course the awesome truth is that the Tabernacle is no longer actually needed, but it helps to explain how God's big story all holds together.

For full details of the Tabernacle, I recommend you visit the website www.domini.org/tabern/

Also check out the Tabernacle on the *Illumina* Bible reference CD-ROM.

Here are some ideas to get you going.

The Laver –

The priests had to wash their hands and feet before entering the sanctuary or making an offering at the altar. Washing in the New Testament also refers to 'washing of the Word'; reading scripture day and night, corresponding to the twice daily ceremonial washing of the Old Testament.

Set up a bowl of water (the laver was a bronze basin, so the more solid the better) and ask folks to think about what dirt has accumulated on their hands over the course of the last few days. What unhelpful attitudes or actions do we allow to build up like dirt on our hands? What are the obvious marks, but also what are the hidden pieces of grime that we might need a nail brush for?

Also read a passage of scripture to underline the daily 'washing of the Word'.

Altar of burnt offering –
Here the priests brought animals without blemish to be sacrificed. Their bloodshed is analogous to Christ's blood, shed for us by the true 'spotless lamb'. Through this sacrifice the sins of the priests and the people would be forgiven. Some explanation regarding the concept of blood sacrifices probably helps at this point.

You could create an altar from some boxes and sticks, and use it as a set-piece to focus minds on what these sacrifices meant. Folks could write the things that they need to sacrifice to God on pieces of wood, and leave them on the altar.

Holy place and holy of holies –
This is a useful way of conveying how privileged we are to have access to God 24 hours a day, 365 days a year. Set up a curtain of some description with Bible verses about 'access' pinned to it. As someone reads the verses and prepares to symbolically step through the veil, get folks to tie a rope around their feet. This echoes what the priests had to do for the high priest in case he was killed stone dead by the glory of God.

Conveying the seriousness of what was going on, while reiterating our new and living way helps to give a sense of the immensity of what Christ achieved. After reading the verses, folks may step through the veil to the holy of holies, which could be maintained as a place of complete silence, to offer worship and just bask in God's glory at the end of the whole process.

[Fusion]

One of my current passions is fusing band-led worship with DJ-led worship; trying to break down the barriers between the two and fuel understanding between the folks in both camps.

If you have them, I'd really encourage you to get your band leaders and DJs together to discuss ways of working together. I will admit, it does take a bit of preparation and a bit of musical know-how but you can't start learning until you try something.

Here is a great example of the two working together fantastically.

Lee '2turntables' Jackson was working with us and we had been passing the leadership back and forwards between us during worship sessions. Lee played me a great track he had found that was a remix of the Coldplay track 'Clocks'. It had a great breakbeat and then that catchy piano intro kicked in. Breakbeats work really well for a lot of modern worship songs, and for some reason this one fitted brilliantly under 'Beautiful One' by Tim Hughes.

People were able to sing something familiar while we were encouraging them to loosen up and get dancing. Lee sampled a bar of the rhythm and let it run under the song till I gave him a nod and he landed the rest of the track on top.

Spontaneously everyone's hands leapt into the air in worship, as the euphoric piano riff changed the mood. People were dancing more freely now, and speaking, shouting or singing their own words up to God. I was able to keep singing some stuff from 'Beautiful One' and some of those beautiful hummed falsetto lines from the Coldplay track, including the refrain 'Home, home, where I long to be'.

You could tell that everyone on the floor knew exactly where that home was. Lee kept coaxing folks to give up their words of worship as we entered the breakdown section – more hands in the air again and more measured specific prayers from folks. Gradually the energy built up as the beat came back in stages until there was a great explosion into 'full pelt'. By this stage the drums were playing too, and some great lead guitar lines were being shredded. All this arced back into a chorus of 'Beautiful One', and although I'm not sure how long the journey took I know it was fabulous.

Mouths

[Sweet And Sour]

This exercise is ideal for a worship time centred on God's presence in the good times and the bad, with our worship being a choice as opposed to a feeling. You could use Matt Redman's song 'Blessed be the Name of the Lord'.

During the song, or as an introduction to it, pass around bowls of sugar and bowls of salt. Read out the passages from the early chapters of Job that touch on the theme or sections from Ecclesiastes 9.

Get folks to taste the sugar, explaining that we may worship at *sweet* times of our lives. Give thanks to God for the things about our lives that are good, and remember the sweetness of the taste and the moment.

Then taste the salt, explaining we are also called to worship at the *sour* times of our lives and that God is no less present at those times. Try to remember both sensations and the fact that you are worshipping during both. If there are specific positive or negative situations in the group, then it may be appropriate to share and address them. Through it all, keep the emphasis on the worship continuing.

p.s. Marking the bowls clearly is always helpful!

[Trinity Talking]

Focus on one point of God's overall story. The most accessible example for this purpose is the cross.

Ask people to get into groups of three, then set the scene. In this case, you could read portions of Psalm 22, which Jesus amazingly invoked on the cross many hundreds of years after the words were written by David. You could also show pictures of the crucifixion. An ambient track may help create the space for people to think and pray.

Now ask each of the three people to play a role in the story. One person takes the role of God the Father, one takes the role of God the Son, and the other takes the role of God the Holy Spirit. Each should speak the words that they believe were being spoken at this moment in history. Suggest that folks pray and ask for truth and wisdom in their words. You may have to use the example of a strong group to encourage the others. The Son – 'Why have you turned your back on me?' The Father – 'My precious son, my precious son.' The Spirit – 'I move through you, I breathe in you, I give you your last breath.' Each person will address different statements to each of the other two persons, and also offer generic cries. Let these thoughts and words become prayers and worship. Once people have persisted beyond the initial pain barrier of doing this, these sessions have been amongst the most poignant and revealing of any worship sessions I have seen.

We live in such a self-centred generation that any activity that snatches us away to see someone else's perspective, especially God's perspective, is very helpful. There is a depth to what occurs because in trying to articulate the words of the Father, Son and Holy Spirit we inevitably catch a glimpse of their heart and heartbreak.

Other moments that you could zoom in on include Jesus' baptism, Pentecost and the Resurrection.

[What If Jesus Hadn't Come?]

This is an interesting thought to throw into a worship session. We often take our New Covenant status for granted. The young people I know are much keener to know about the New Testament than the Old, which means we can lose track of whose shoulders we stand on and the privileged position we hold.

There are so many things that would be different in us, in our worship and in our world if Jesus had not come.

Here are some that young people have come up with previously, to get you thinking.

> *We would still be sacrificing animals, and only the High Priest would really meet with you. We would have a second-hand experience.*

> *My life would be completely worse, without the changes you have made.*

The last 2000 years of history would have been so different. I think the world would be even crazier and barbaric. Think of the Christians who abolished slavery. And Martin Luther King.

We would still be Gentiles. I enjoy being one of your 'chosen people'\.

We would still be living in BC. Oh, no, we wouldn't actually. Umm ...

An alternative dramatic way to make the same point is to read the Christmas readings, but change some endings so the stable is bare when the shepherds arrive, or Herod is successful in his purge. I know it's extreme, but it sometimes takes something like that to snap me out of my sloppy attitude to the miracle that Jesus is.

I would suggest asking folks to think in silence about what would be different, and then let this flow into a time of spoken worship, where each prayer begins. 'Jesus, if you hadn't come ...'

[Acapella]

There seems to be something special about singing acapella (i.e. without music). Everything else is stripped away, and everyone knows that any sense of wonder is coming from God's presence and the simple beauty of melody and harmony; not from an impressive band. A path is cleared for deeper intimacy when you can easily hear your own voice communicating directly with God, and you feel supported in a vocal sense by others around you. This is a parable in itself.

Singing in this way also challenges everyone's perceptions about when and where they can worship by singing. They can do it walking home, in the bath, or while surfing the net. Once you have tried it without the 'safety net' it is much easier to step onto the tightrope in the future.

The most effective times of acapella singing are when everyone is lifting their voices to full volume, but this is hard to engender when folks do not have the confidence of much noise or support around them. So a good plan is to build up the intensity of the song, perhaps with an extra loud chorus, making it clear that you are going to be repeating the chorus. Then as everyone starts singing the next chorus, pull out any instruments, to leave the voices ringing out on their own.

During acapella singing it may sometimes be helpful to stomp a foot, or thump a guitar, to keep everyone in rhythm. The timing of the leader's singing in these times is as important as the pitch and quality of her voice. Sometimes you may want to release a drummer to play creatively over the singing, which may take you to a different place altogether for the next song.

Here are some song sections that work well acapella –

- Holy, Holy, Holy is the Lord God Almighty
- I love you Lord (and I lift my voice)
- Purify my Heart – chorus
- Amazing Grace
- You are God in Heaven – chorus
- Salvation Belongs to our God – chorus
- Great is the Darkness – chorus
- Great is the Lord – chorus
- Hallelujah, my Father
- He is the Lord – chorus
- Jesus, Jesus, Holy and Anointed One
- Hallelujah (your love is amazing) – slow chorus

[Mountain Tops]

Quite simply this is a phenomenal passage to read at the start of a time of worship. It's even more effective if a DJ is gradually cranking up a track as the reading gains momentum, or a drummer/percussionist is slowly building a rhythm. Either read Hebrews 12:18–29 straight through, or select verses 18–19, 22–25 and 26–29 as separate sections to be read between the verses of a song while gradually increasing the intensity. The powerful contrast between Sinai and Zion perfectly encapsulates the privilege of worshipping in New Covenant times. The phrase 'see to it that you do not refuse him who speaks' also never fails to hit home powerfully.

You may want to use some visual imagery of mountains, or create a 'mountain top' feel with a backdrop. You could get people to share experiences of reaching the summits of mountains. Ask what they saw, and how they felt, and what it felt like on the way back down. In what ways was it similar/not similar to meeting with God?

[Jesus, Your Love] – (*Distinctive Sounds* – ICC)

Find as many mirrors as you can. Get folks to stare long and hard at themselves. When we struggle to love ourselves, it's hard to let God love us. Do we like what we see 1) on the outside or 2) on the inside? Do we love what we see?

This song was written from a place where many young people are, trapped by serious insecurity and a belief that they're not worth anything. Perhaps read scriptures that focus on God loving us in the midst of our humanity. Romans 5:8, for example: 'While we were still sinners, Christ died for us.'

A key line in the song is 'You know me, yet you love me.' It may be worth leading a meditation on how completely God knows us – every thought, motive, and action; yet still he loves us. You could use Psalm 139.

When using this song we often repeat the last line of the chorus a few times, singing 'oh, how I need your love' several times. In an age when self-sufficiency is programmed into us, it is often hard (for older teenagers especially) to admit that we need anyone. You may have to encourage this process of 'coming to him as a little child.'

Q: When was the last time you stopped for long enough to let God love you?

[Headlines]

As an inspiration to worship, find some contemporary stories of God at work; whether in a miraculous healing, a cultural shift, an attitude change or a supernatural event. Present them in a way that folks will find familiar, whether through a news bulletin or mock headlines in a newspaper, drawing the parallel that these events are just as real as the news we watch but are often just not reported. Use a song like 'You are Mighty' in response. The magazine *Faith for Life* has a monthly section called 'Good News Does Happen' that is a good resource for this sort of thing.

An alternative or addition is to mock up headlines from Bible stories so that they have a larger impact than normal – 'Pharaoh's army all washed up', for example. After showing a few of yours, encourage the group to write their own. Hopefully this reinforces the reality of these events and their connection through time to us. These things didn't happen in another world. They happened in this world. As everyone reads each other's headlines, let the reality of the stories inspire people into worship.

[Committed To Memory]
Encouraging folks to memorise the words of a simple song such as 'I love you, Lord' can powerfully change the dynamic from word-reading and thinking, to focusing on the spiritual, what we are doing with our bodies and the space we are in. It brings a powerful sense of freedom.

[Holy Ground]
What places do we regard as 'holy' ground? What sort of places would we not be allowed to enter? Where would we have to take extreme care?

Read Exodus 3:1–6

Encourage everyone to take off their shoes as part of their worship. You could also use the awesome visuals of a burning bush on One Small Barking Dog's new video/DVD 'Images 4'. There is a sample to download from www.youthwork.co.uk/resources/.

Use the song 'Holy Ground' (*The Source*).

Take time to listen to what God may have to say.

[Thirsty]
An obvious, but very powerful idea. Invite folks to come forward during the song 'All who are Thirsty' to drink from glasses of water, or have water splashed on them. This has been particularly powerful at times when a group has not met for some time, and individuals are feeling dry and thirsty for God.

[Heart's Desire Balloons]
This is a strong and memorable visual image, which helpfully cements an important promise into memory.

Read Psalm 37:4 – 'Delight yourself in the Lord, and he will give you the desires of your heart.'

Take some time to pray and honestly assess what your heart's desires are. If needs be, discuss it with a friend who knows you well.

Write them down on a small piece of paper and poke it into a balloon.

Think about what it means for you to 'delight yourself in the Lord'. What brings you delight? Does God do that for you too? If not, do we need to enjoy God a bit more than we allow ourselves to?

Blow up the balloon to symbolise God working and breathing his spirit into your desire. Or even better, use helium!

Keep everyone's balloons in a suitable receptacle. Hold on to them as you pray about your heart's desires, and then literally let go of it to God. If you're getting really adventurous, release them outside, with your home address attached to the bottom so that someone can post it back to you. Have a competition to see whose balloon has made it the furthest – p.s. there is absolutely no spiritual analogy to the competition.

OT: Eden – YFC Gillingham

IDEAS

IDEAS

Eyes And Ears

[Video clips]

As mentioned earlier, this is a visually stimulated generation that learns through story so for a long time now movie clips have been used as a vital part of preaching and teaching. Sadly there is less use of them in the context of worship. There are many clips that lend themselves well to being used. You just have to look out for them. Drawing analogy or contrast between characters or situations and the truth about the God we worship is effective in inspiring young people to appreciate aspects of God's character.

Some examples to get you going:

1. *The Truman Show*: when Truman finally meets his maker. Contrast the controlling, abusing, stuck-in-an-ivory-tower 'creator' Christoph, with the freeing, loving, incarnational God that we worship. Use it with 'Light of the World' by Tim Hughes.

2. *Saving Private Ryan*: when Ryan is wondering if he's lived a good enough life to repay Tom Hanks' character for what he did for him. It's a powerful meditation that can be woven into songs on grace.

3. *Jesus of Nazareth*: many excellent sections, but none better than the telling of the Prodigal Son story. Use it with 'Open Arms'.

4. *The Miracle Maker*: when the camera carries us at speed from the cross into the holy of holies. What better pictorial way into worship is there than that?

5. *28 Days Later*: when the main character wanders through a deserted London but ends up at the foot of a cross. A chilling but memorable introduction to a time of sung worship. Links to 'In Christ Alone'.

6. *Amelie*: when she performs random acts of kindness for her fellow townsfolk. Again a great link to grace.

[Quotes]

Quotes can be very effective when used in the right context, particularly in our soundbite-obsessed culture. To slot into a worship context snugly, you could ask that a group take a few Bible chapters and list all the quotes therein about Jesus, or God. You could also allow some artistic licence away from the text for what they believe different characters would have said, had they been interviewed for TV news, straight after their encounters with Jesus.

Another way of splitting the group is for folks to take one Bible character each. Leave the sets of quotes looping on a screen, or place them on boards around a room.

You can download a quotes presentation from www.youthwork. co.uk/resources/.

The web is a great place to find quotes about anything! Simply search in Google for 'quote *XX*', where *XX* is your required theme, and you are there.

A good transatlantic site is http://www.hopecrc.ca/quotes.htm

[Joining With Creation]

Matt Redman's song 'Let Ev'rything That' is a standard with many groups and churches, and one day while singing it God quite specifically spoke to me about the words of the second verse: 'Praise you on the earth now, joining with creation, calling all the nations to your praise.'

It struck me that we sometimes have a pretty blinkered view of creation's praising God. We acknowledge the trees of the fields clapping their hands, the rocks crying out, and the wide span of creation itself reflecting the glory of God, but I realised that I had never sung those words aware that the high point of that creation, which I was joining with, was standing right beside me.

As humans we come together to worship, but so often we don't even acknowledge each other's existence. We stare straight ahead at the words, or zip up our eyes to enter our personal worship tunnel.

If you travel a bit around the world, you find that this is predominantly a problem in the West. Even our worship experiences have been privatised.

So I often find myself cajoling people into making some serious eye contact as they sing that section – still worshipping, but acknowledging the horizontal dimension to what is going on. Often it will take a few attempts to get past what I call the 'giggle phase', but it is worth persisting, with confidence. Don't let initial inertia dampen your enthusiasm to make it work.

It is amazing how this has often been a turning point in a worship time. God breaks down barriers between people, so that they can worship in unity. He moves.

[Creation]

A 'choreographed' MS PowerPoint presentation alongside a reading of Genesis 1 is always very powerful if shots of the stars and the sun etc. appear at appropriate moments. A slowly building ambient track is also excellent for this, such as 'Offshore' by Chicane (*Far from the Maddening Crowd*).

These are very easy to assemble from Microsoft wallpaper slides and any number of images available on the net. You could also use songs such 'Maker of all Things'.

Visit the website to download the Genesis 1 presentation. Or go to www.highwayvideo.com for fantastic CD-ROM videos on creation; 'NATURAL' on vibe3, and 'GALAXY' on vibe2.

[Zoo Worship]

This idea connects really strongly with a ZOO TV generation. Strong single words impact our consciousness, especially when they are springing from, contrasting with or describing another medium that is simultaneously being used.

The idea is to introduce some scripture and then get young people to dissect what that actually says about God.

Here is an example using Psalm 23. Someone reads the text of the Psalm while a screen is flashing the words in capitals at the indicated moments.

Psalm 23:1–6

The Lord is my shepherd, [**RELATIONSHIP**] *I shall not be in want.* [**SUPPLY**]
He makes me lie down in green pastures, [**REST**]
he leads me beside quiet waters, [**REFRESHMENT**]
he restores my soul. [**HEALING**]
He guides me in paths of righteousness [**GUIDANCE**]
for his name's sake. [**PURPOSE**]

> *Even though I walk*
> *through the valley of the shadow of death,* [**REALITY**]
> *I will fear no evil,*
> *for you are with me;* [**COURAGE**]
> *your rod and your staff,*
> *they comfort me.* [**PROTECTION**]
> *You prepare a table before me*
> *in the presence of my enemies.* [**HOPE**]
> *You anoint my head with oil;* [**SPIRIT**
> *my cup overflows.* [**ENOUGH**]
> *Surely goodness and love will follow me*
> *all the days of my life,* [**BLESSING**]
> *and I will dwell in the house of the Lord* [**SECURITY**]
> *for ever.* [**ETERNITY**]

This is very effective as an introduction into a time of sung worship, as you can then leave the words in capitals cycling.

As you can imagine, the possibilities are endless. Try the same exercise with other Bible passages, and you will see how helpful this crystallisation process can be.

Variations
Write out a large version of the Bible passage you wish to use. Stick this up on a suitably large wall, then invite the young people to use paint or thick red pen to add single words summarising the character of God from each phrase or set of phrases. Alternatively, you can list all the blessings for us that are described in that section. Again, these words should be somewhere that is still in view when you enter a time of sung worship.

[Tracks]
The added impact of using commercially available tracks is that in the future when a young person hears that track again on television or the radio, there is a resonance back to the worship experience. Thinking God-thoughts is becoming part of normal life. We all know this phenomenon from being able to remember where we were on a journey when specific songs were on the radio. Keep your ears open for them. Here are a few examples.

Why Does My Heart Feel So Bad?

This is track 4 on Moby's CD *PLAY*. Fade up the track from about 1 minute and wait for the beginning of the female vocal before reading Psalm 42 over the top of the track. The psalm splits nicely into two sections, taking a break when the lead vocal returns. The longing of the psalm 'Why are you so sad, O my soul?' resonates perfectly with the feel and lyric of the track. You could project the words from the psalm to help people focus.

This is often a good way of introducing people who aren't used to worship. The universally known track and the universal feeling of life not going too well provide important common ground for the start of their journey.

Grace

This beautiful track is from the album *All that you Can't Leave Behind* by U2. It is very useful in a communion setting, alongside people sharing stories about

1 bad things that have happened to them that they didn't deserve,
2 good things that have happened to them that they didn't deserve.

Suggest to everyone that this week they do one thing for one other person which they don't deserve. Be grace.

Walk on

From the same album, the inspirational track about heaven and earth works fantastically well with Bible verses that refer to 'walking' looping on a screen. It is a good track to use if folks are quite literally walking around the room, looking at the words or pictures that others have written on rolls of paper or other media, perhaps earlier in an event.

An alternative is scribbling out lots of quotes beforehand for people to view as they wander around a room. They have the freedom to move quickly between them, or just meditate on a couple.

The PowerPoint presentation is on www.youthwork.co.uk/resources/.

139

An amazing track for transition into worship is '139' by YFC band Dependance. It is a cracking dance track with an eastern feel, incorporating a modern translation of Psalm 139 prayed passionately as the music ebbs and flows. Combined with a simple PowerPoint presentation of the words, it is a very powerful way of encouraging folks to let God search their hearts at the beginning of a time of sung worship.

An MP3 and PowerPoint are available for download on the site www.youthwork.co.uk/resources/.

On this theme, you can also display images like fingerprints that underline our uniqueness and how completely God knows us. Read Luke 12:7 – 'Even the very hairs on your head are numbered'. The fingerprint image is also on the website.

[Bring And Sing]

Get everyone to bring a track that inspires them to worship. This may or may not be a 'worship' track, and may not be performed or written by a Christian. Ask folks to first explain why they chose this track specifically, and what it is about it that inspires them. Where possible encourage folks to 'enter in' and share the experience that one of the group is providing. That may mean singing along, or thanking God in prayer for what is evoked by a track. A quick tip here is to stagger this exercise over two or three weeks, as inevitably it takes a while to listen to everyone's tracks and explanations.

[Downtime]

It is often very effective to provide some downtime, especially in the midst of songs that focus on the cross (e.g. 'Jesus Christ' (once again), 'Here I am to Worship' (breakdown section), 'Surrender').

Endowing a young worship band with the nerve and licence to move into sections of freer worship like this is a difficult task, but one that is worth persisting with.

Choose a short 4-bar section from a song (such as those mentioned above) or any other section that has a sense of movement to it (usually via a moving bass line). Get the band to learn this short chunk, playing it repeatedly until they can confidently do it without reference to music. Encourage them to focus on their actual playing or singing as being worship to God, rather than depending on only using words. It is good to play the section a few times without any words to leave the freedom for singers or others to supplant these with their own words, which may be personal, or may strike a theme that everyone can then follow. In the midst of this, you may need to encourage the band to also think about musical dynamics, to mirror what is happening spiritually.

[Audio Samples]

We are using more and more snippets of preachers in the course of worship. Sometimes it takes a bit of effort to hunt down old seminar tapes, but it is worth it once you find a gem. Spoken truth in the context of worship is so powerful. The CD/DVD *1 GIANT LEAP* is a great example of words mixed with music to stunning effect.

Those who are into DJ-ing are the best folks to run with this idea. Encourage them to get hold of tapes and CDs of preachers and record small usable sections for 'dropping in' to worship sessions. These could be triggered from a CD player or a simple sampler.

Clips we use regularly include 'My King – He's Indescribable' by Pastor Loughridge during the song 'King of Kings, Majesty', and soundbites of Brennan Manning speaking about God's unconditional love during songs about grace.

Sometimes the symbiosis of song, music and spoken word produces something more significant than the sum of its parts. The most powerful recent example of this happened at Greenbelt. We had been leading a worship session based around trade justice issues, praying for justice and equality around the world. The final song we used was 'Holy, holy'. Even though it was early morning there was a real intensity to what was happening, and the large crowd lifted their voices to sing unaccompanied. It was a special moment; and then suddenly the voice of Martin Luther King was booming out: 'I have a dream that one day every valley shall be exalted, that every hill and mountain shall be made low. The rough places will be made plain and the crooked places will be made straight, and the Glory of the Lord shall be revealed and all flesh shall see it together.'

No one moved as the reality of what God's holiness looked like in the flesh was underlined to us all. It felt as if heaven and earth had met.

Fingers

[A to Z]
The alphabet is a very useful tool as a framework for worship.

Put up 26 large pieces of paper all around a hall and get folks to write or draw things for which they are thankful to God on the appropriate sheet. For example, 'food' and 'friends' under F. I have had people write 'xylem' under X. I guess there are always are some keen Year 9 biologists.

Similarly, you can use each sheet to write words that describe God beginning with each letter – G for giver, glorious, gracious, etc.

Or...

In the midst of a strongly rhythmic worship time encourage folks to shout out a letter and then everyone joins in with words to describe God which begin with that letter. If folks are slow to initiate you can just work through the alphabet, with the leader announcing the start of a new letter.

[Writing Tomorrow's Headlines]
Recently it struck me that too often we settle for the world we are presented with, instead of fighting for it to be different. We see the news as being about something out there, somehow dissociated from us. More worryingly, we are numbed into thinking that we cannot do anything to change the headlines. I observe this sense of dissociation and apathy in many young people, who believe that only by appearing on television can they achieve significance but it seems too far away to bother with.

This is a helpful exercise for encouraging teenagers to step into the prophetic and intercessory worlds in a way that they can understand. The premise is simple. You get to write the world's headlines. There are many ways to break this down to keep it interesting for everyone.

Time: Some people could work on tomorrow's headlines, some on next week's, some on next year's, and others on headlines 10, 50, 100 years into the future. It focuses the mind slightly if you give them something like 3 June 2045 as a specific date.

Location: Some folks could be working on *The New York Times* while others could be working on *The Sydney Morning Herald* or *Iraq Daily News*.

Theme: It might help to suggest areas that they may want to address – poverty, war, revival, drugs, murder, sport.

Ask everyone to pray before they begin, asking God for what he would love to see in all the different areas of life. Perhaps explain that as well as headlines like 'One Million become Christians' God is interested in seeing the renewal of every area of society.

Create lots of newspaper-sized pieces of paper for the headlines to be printed onto, or use old newspapers with headlines stuck on top. Then encourage everyone to wander around the room praying that these things come to pass. Explain that seeing future hope, where the world can see none, is a key part of intercession and hearing God's heart.

It may help to use a song such as 'The Spirit of the Sovereign Lord'. One line in this song is particularly applicable – 'because he has anointed us to preach good news'. As well as the good news we know from the Bible, we have a role in speaking hope and potential good news into people's lives.

[Affirmation]

This is another healthily counter-cultural exercise. As there is not a lot of encouragement or affirmation out there for young people, criticism has become our mother tongue in many ways. Blessing and encouraging each other is a really good habit to get into in the context of worship. Sometimes eye contact and a safe hug are all that are needed to communicate, but words always help. Here are some ideas if the words don't flow easily.

Read 1 Thessalonians 5:11 – 'Therefore encourage one another.'

Stick a bit of paper on everyone's back. Then as people move around you can write something you like about each person, behind their back.

Alternatively, get everyone to write their name on the top of a piece of paper and then pass the sheets clockwise around the group. The concept is like the game consequences. Write your encouraging sentence for the person whose name is on the top of the sheet, then fold it over and pass it on. Watch out for the smiles when the sheets get back to their owners.

In larger gatherings, postcards are an excellent way of enabling people to minister to each other. During a time of sung worship, distribute three or four postcards to every person in the room. They write their encouragement on the card and deliver it to the recipient. People may have a strong sense that God wants to say specific things to specific people, or simply want to encourage each other by pointing out how their lives are a blessing. Sadly, sometimes this will be the only time that young people hear this sort of stuff, so the fact that the words are written down as a permanent record is very helpful. Spoken encouragement is vital, but can be drowned out by the noise of the world after a few hours. Never underestimate the power of things that young people can keep. This is something that could become a regular part of worship sessions, so that an atmosphere of encouragement is created.

Sometimes questions are helpful to get the encouragement juices flowing, as we have been so conditioned into being blind to people's attributes but vigilant for their faults.

- Who from this group would you really miss if they weren't here?
- Is there anyone here who is taken for granted?
- What is their finest quality?
- Have they encouraged you in the past?
- What things have they done for you that you have never thanked them for?
- Is there something about them that inspires you to be better at something?
- Do you think anyone here just needs to know that God loves them?
- Is there anyone who needs to know that God has their future sorted?

[Txt Worship]
Use a mobile phone number that you don't mind everyone knowing. Give out this number as a base station for folks to text prayers and thanks to. It is best to have the number on a screen or poster. Stress that it is not a race, but a useful way of prioritising what you want to say to God. You've basically got about 160 characters to say what is most on your heart. Enjoy the cacophony as message after message pours in. Get folks to think about what it must be like in heaven, receiving messages from all over the planet. Then read out the txt-bits of worship for everyone to shout 'Amen' or 'Yes' at the top of their voices, or display them in PowerPoint.

As an introduction to this exercise, it is fun to do a txt quiz. In this you ask a question that has a longish answer, such as: 'What is the correct spelling of the name of England's football manager?' The winner is the first person who gets a correct txt to the central phone. This creates a lot of excitement as those well-practised thumbs get a work-out. The beauty of this game is what happens next. Get everyone in the room deathly silent, then call the winning number back to see whose phone rings (remind them to turn their ringtones onto loud).

[Few words]
Read Ecclesiastes 5:1–3, which includes the phrase 'let my words be few'. Give each person three pieces of paper. Tell them to write one word only on each sheet: 1) a word that describes God, 2) a word that says how they feel about God, and 3) a word that asks something of God. Leave space for folks to sit and contemplate, perhaps using Matt Redman's 'You are God in Heaven' in the background. Keep the emphasis on simplicity. Then when each person has decided on their words, they leave them scattered on the floor. Everyone can then move around, reading each other's words, and worship through those too.

[Names for God]
Get people to write names for God or aspects of his character on a blank acetate sheet, perhaps as a simple song is being sung. Use different colours and don't just write them in a list. Very soon the sheet will be filled with words flowing in every direction that will give people an excellent touchstone during any worship time, as often our worship can focus on only one of God's attributes, e.g.

his love, to the detriment of thinking about his whole character. You could invite someone to share a testimony, and then ask folks to describe the God they see in action in that story.

[Fingerprints]
There is something special about adding your fingerprint to something, as no one else can make a mark quite like yours. This can be used in many ways:

1 Asking people to put their fingerprints on a large white cross to show their identification with Christ or to admit their individual sin.
2 Drawing a picture of a human body with the prints to focus on unity in diversity.
3 Adding your fingerprint to a map as a sign of praying for an area, underlining the unique impact of your prayer.

[Poems]
There are many young people who feel disenfranchised by contemporary youth worship culture as they have no desire to sing, and cannot connect with most of the music. However it is amazing how many of these people will scribe heartfelt poetry in private moments. In my experience folks often presume the poets amongst them are daydreaming and doodling, when something much deeper may actually be going on. For some reason poetry seems to be an outlet for those who struggle to find other outlets. Please hear what I am saying here. Not all poets are recluses, but from the point of view of the youth worker theirs is one of the most likely giftings to be missed because of its oft-associated shyness.

Encourage people to share what they have written bit by bit and then gradually include their poems in worship sessions. Next you may want to ask people to write poems specifically for a certain session, on a certain theme. This focus may well help their creative juices to flow, and may also direct their writing to be more inclusive and helpful to the whole group. Poems set to instrumental music can be particularly powerful.

[How Does It Feel?]
Thanks for this idea go to Emma Duncan, a youth worker in Bristol. She used my song 'How does it Feel?' (from the albums *Advertising*

the Invisible and *Spring Harvest Evolution*), but any track focusing on the cross could work. 'How does it feel?' is a worship song with a bit of twist, in that it is asking God how it felt in those horrendous moments on the cross. It is about trying to get your head around the craziness of God becoming a man, and all the shame that entailed. The words of the chorus are

> *How does it feel?*
> *To be ruler of all and then subject to evil.*
> *How does it feel?*
> *To be strung up for all to see.*

After singing the song, Emma got her crew to write down what they thought Jesus may have been experiencing and thinking during those moments. They then sang it again, with these thoughts in mind. I recommend it as an exercise. You may be surprised at the depth and breadth of what comes back.

Here are some of the things people have written:

> *'I cry for you, I fear for you. Fear for what you do to yourselves. But most of all, I want you to see what I have done for you.'*

> *'The worst bit is knowing I have to be without my Father. Knowing he won't be able to look at me carrying your sins. I have never been apart from him before. I have never left his side or known a day in eternity without his constant presence, love and protection.'*

> *'I feel like people are all watching me. Waiting for me to do something to prove who I am ... I'm wishing there was another way... '*

> *'I love you so much. I love you beyond reason or human logic. I love you with a passion that leaves me breathless on the cross.'*

To Basics

Having surveyed the wide landscape of worship for this distinctive generation, it should be noted that most of the time there are no sound systems, no clever images, no artistic responses and not more than a few young people.

If this situation rings true for you, then I desperately want to encourage you as to the significance of what you are doing in these scenarios even though it may often feel that you are seeing little fruit from your labours. There may not be stage-splitting moves of God or tongues of fire alighting on everyone's head, but what you are sowing in the lives of the young people by your very desire to be there is incredibly important.

God is not sitting in heaven awarding points like a judge in some Eurovision Worship Contest. I am certain he couldn't care less whether or not we are still using last year's songs. More than anything, he just wants us to show up. Sometimes it won't feel spectacular, but that is the backbone of a real life with God.

I'll be forever thankful for the people who taught me (both intentionally and unintentionally) to worship. It happened in cold, grimy church halls where there was as much atmosphere as a party on the surface of the moon. It happened on nasty plastic seats that never had all four legs the same length. It happened with the aid of a Casio keyboard that gave everything that bossa nova feel while sounding like an overpriced xylophone. It happened with a repertoire of about 15 songs. It happened even though my guitar playing bore more resemblance to Eric Bristow than Eric Clapton.

The bottom line is, it happened. Man looks on the outward appearance but the Lord looks at the heart. My amazing leaders (Alan, Billy and Keith) were never going to win a Grammy, but they were there.

He doesn't need us to be impressive. The Father simply asks us to stand on the roof with him for a few moments so we can look out and understand where his lost ones are running home from.

Let's go meet them, and walk home together.

Youthwork the partnership

ALOVE (The Salvation Army for a new generation), Oasis, Spring Harvest, Youth for Christ and *Youthwork magazine* are working together to equip and resource the church for effective youthwork and ministry.

The partnership exists to offer support, encouragement and ideas for busy youth workers including:

Youthwork the conference

Youthwork the conference is a weekend event designed for church-based volunteer youth workers, with specific streams for younger leaders and salaried youth workers. *Youthwork the conference* has been designed to give training and support by offering encouragement, ideas and resources to busy youth workers. There is also an additional early day conference specifically for full time youth workers.

The conference includes:

Main plenary sessions with teaching, worship, prayer, reflection and encouragement plus many practical and skills based seminars covering a wide range of youthwork issues. You'll also find opportunities to network with others and space to reflect and pray as well as access to a large range of youth ministry specialist agencies via an extensive exhibition and resource area.

Youthwork the conference takes place each November. Visit www.youthwork.co.uk/conference or call 0870 060 3327 for more information.

Youthwork the conference is administrated by Spring Harvest.

Youthwork magazine

Since 1992, *Youthwork magazine* has been the magazine of choice for youth workers across the UK. Every issue is packed with resources, information and opinion, provid-  ing youth workers with all the latest news on youth ministry and youth culture. Each month there are book, album and resource reviews, challenging and inspiring articles, Jobsearch, must-see websites, and a pull-out section packed with ready-to-use curriculum resources including drama, discussion triggers, and ways to use music and film with your group. With all this and more jammed into every issue, it's no surprise that so many youth workers consider *Youthwork magazine* essential reading.

On sale in most Christian bookshops. Visit www.youthwork. co.uk/magazine or call 01892 652364 for more information or to subscribe.

Youthwork magazine is published by CCP Limited.

Youthwork the resources

A series of books to help you in your youth-work and ministry, in three categories. *Developing Practice* titles are designed for all those engaged in youthwork and ministry. They are inspirational and practical without being overtly theoretical. *Going Deeper* titles are designed for those who are serious about youthwork and ministry. They are sometimes controversial, always challenging, but never dogmatic. *Resourcing Ministry* titles provide busy youth workers with tried and tested ideas and curriculum to use with their young people.

Visit www.youthwork.co.uk/resources or call 01825 769111 for more information.

Youthwork the resources are published by Spring Harvest Publishing.

Youthwork the training

What Every Volunteer Youth Worker Should Know

YOUTHWORK
the training

A training course for busy 'extra timers' who need to know the basics – and fast! This innovative course provides a foundation of knowledge, tips and resources in an accessible and practical format. The course is made up of 9 two-hour sessions which may be delivered in a variety of ways to fit your needs and lifestyle! You can choose when and where you do the sessions.

Participation includes a free resource book and 100 ready-to-use ideas. The course is endorsed by a broad spectrum of Christian denominations and networks.

Visit www.youthwork.co.uk/training/volunteerscourse or call 0207 450 9044 for more information.

'What Every Volunteer Youthworker Should Know' is managed and delivered by Oasis.

The Art of Connecting

A resource to equip you and your youth group to see lives changed ... forever! The vision behind 'The Art of Connecting' is the realisation that people communicate most naturally when they are exploring their own stories together. The course aims to empower people to share their faith through story – making connections between their story, their friends' stories and God's story.

'The Art of Connecting' book and Leaders Pack are available, as are regional training days for youth leaders and young people.

Visit www.youthwork.co.uk/training/aoc or call 0121 550 8055 for more information.

'The Art of Connecting' is developed and delivered by Youth for Christ.

Youthwork online

www.youthwork.co.uk features a dynamic home page updated weekly with the latest information, news analysis and views on youthwork and youth culture – all things  that will be of interest to you in your work with young people. It's also the place to find out about the partnership and how we can support you, including more details on the conference, magazine, training courses, and resources.

At www.youthwork.co.uk/community you'll also find a range of online discussion forums where you can discuss youth ministry issues and share ideas and resources with other youth workers from across the country.

Visit www.youthwork.co.uk for more information.

Youthwork online is owned by CCP Limited and developed by all the partners.

Oasis develops effective ways of transforming the lives of the poor and marginalised and whole communities in the UK and around the world. We help churches and individuals do the same.

Drawing on 20 years experience of pioneering mission, education and youthwork initiatives; Oasis provides opportunities for young people to participate in life changing UK and Global mission on both a short and long term basis and equips youth workers with innovative resources and training including the 'What Every Volunteer Youth Worker Should Know' course & the JNC-qualifying Oasis Youth Work and Ministry Degree.

Oasis also enables youth workers and church volunteers to support young people's personal, social and health education in their local schools through training associate educators in sex and relationships education and mentoring as well as tackling social exclusion among young people head on through the delivery of one to one transition work, mentoring and supported housing programmes.

To find out more about Oasis:

Visit: www.oasistrust.org

Email: enquiries@oasistrust.org

Phone: 0207 450 9000

Write to: Oasis, The Oasis Centre, 115 Southwark Bridge Road, London, SE1 0AX, England.

The Salvation Army for a new generation

ALOVE is The Salvation Army for a new generation. ALOVE is calling a generation to dynamic faith, radical lifestyle, adventurous mission and a fight for justice.

ALOVE provides young people and young adults with ongoing opportunities to engage in culturally engaging worship, cell and small group discipleship, innovative mission and world changing social action.

ALOVE runs training programmes to develop leaders and missionaries for the 21st century. ALOVE is also pioneering new expressions of church, youth work and social inclusion in communities around the United Kingdom and Ireland.

To find out more about ALOVE:

Visit: www.salvationarmy.org.uk/ALOVE

Email: ALOVE@salvationarmy.org.uk

Phone: 0208 288 1202

Write to: ALOVE UK, The Salvation Army, 21 Crown Lane, Morden, Surrey, SM4 5BY, England.

Spring Harvest's vision is to 'equip the Church for action'. Through a range of events, conferences, courses and resources Christians are enabled to impact their local communities and the wider world.

Spring Harvest is probably best known for its Main Event, held every Easter, which attracts over 55,000 people of all ages. Over 10,000 of those attending are young people. The Main Event also includes specific streams which cater for over 2,000 students. Alongside the teaching programme, Spring Harvest provide a range of resources for young people and those involved in youth ministry.

Through their sister company – Spring Harvest Holidays – they offer quality holidays at our four-star holiday park in the Vendee, France. These inspirational holidays cater for people of all ages in a safe, secure and relaxed environment.

The Spring Harvest range of resources – albums, books and teaching resources – all aim to equip the church for action.

To find out more about Spring Harvest:

Visit: www.springharvest.org

Email: info@springharvest.org

Phone: 01825 769000

Write to: Spring Harvest, 14 Horsted Square, Uckfield, East Sussex, TN22 1QG, England.

Spring Harvest. A Registered Charity.

Youth for Christ (YFC), one of the most dynamic Christian organisations, are taking good news relevantly to every young person in Britain. They help tackle the big issues facing young people today. They're going out on the streets, into schools and communities and have changed the lives of countless people throughout the UK.

Their staff, trainees and volunteers currently reach over 50,000 young people each week and have over 50 centres in locations throughout the UK. They also provide creative arts and sports mission teams, a network of registered groups and a strong emphasis on 'three-story' evangelism. YFC International works in 120 nations.

To find out more about YFC:

Visit: www.yfc.co.uk

Email: churchresource@yfc.co.uk

Phone: 0121 550 8055

Write to: YFC, PO Box 5254, Halesowen, West Midlands B63 3DG, England.

Youthwork magazine is Britain's most widely read magazine resource for Christian youth workers. Through articles, ready-to-use resources, reviews, youthwork and cultural news and analysis, and much more, *Youthwork magazine* provides ideas, resources and guidance to help you in your work with young people.

Youthwork magazine is published monthly by CCP Limited, which is part of the Premier Media Group, who also publish *Christianity* and *Christian Marketplace*.

To find out more about *Youthwork magazine*:

Visit: www.youthwork.co.uk

Email: youthwork@premier.org.uk

Phone: 01892 652364

Write to: Youthwork Magazine, CCP Limited, Broadway House, The Broadway, Crowborough, TN6 1HQ, England.